True Miracles with Genealogy

Help from Beyond the Veil

Compiled by Anne Bradshaw

True Miracles with Genealogy

Help from Beyond the Veil

© 2010 Anne Bradshaw

Bradshaw, Anne

True Miracles with Genealogy / compiled by Anne Bradshaw

Cover design by Rachael Anderson

ISBN # 1453767118

EAN-13 # 9781453767115

Printed in the United States of America

www.truemiracleswithgenealogy.com

For families everywhere.

May you connect eternally.

Table of Contents

Acknowledgements

Seeing this book finally come together makes me feel like cheering. I am so grateful to everyone who sent in genealogy research stories. Each account is unique. Each is a miracle. Each will inspire readers as they come to the heady realization that family history work is of great consequence, it is powerful, there is a world of spirits, and it really is possible to unite families forever.

I also want to thank Annette Lyon, editor at Precision Editing Group (www.precisioneditinggroup.com), and Rachael Renee Anderson (www.rachaelreneeanderson.com) who designed the book cover. My thanks as always to all my LDStorymakers and Facebook friends. I'd be lost without them. Someone always knows the answer, no matter what a writer needs to know.

In addition, my appreciation goes to Mary E. Petty, B.A. (Genealogy and History), who suggested I create a website and use it as a gathering place for collecting research stories. I jumped at the idea. How exciting to keep on spreading this inspiring information throughout the Internet. The new website is at www.truemiracleswithgenealogy.com.

Two stories from James W. Petty, AG, CG, B.A. (History), B.S.(Genealogy) in this book are but a tiny portion of the miracles he and his wife have experienced during their work as professional genealogists. I'm grateful to them both for their wisdom and knowledge. Their professional genealogy research services company is called Heirlines Family History & Genealogy, Inc. (www.heirlines.com). Readers can contact them at PO Box 893, Salt Lake City, UT, 84110 or by telephone at (800) 570-4049.

Introduction

Who doesn't enjoy a good story? And when that story is true, it is even more compelling. *True Miracles with Genealogy* is a collection of family-history research stories written by ordinary people with extraordinary experiences. These events are part of the reward that comes from doing genealogy. They are the fathers turning their hearts to their children—the spiritual moments as help comes from beyond the veil.

Most of the accounts in this book tell of connections from the other side of the veil that led to amazing discoveries. Others, however, declare how ancestors let descendants know they are still alive, that they care, and that they do not want to be forgotten or misrepresented.

I believe God has a hand in these miracles—that he wants us to unite with our families by seeking out our family trees. In the book of Malachi (4:6), it says, "Behold, I will send you Elijah the prophet . . . And he shall turn the heart of the fathers to the children, and the heart of the children to their fathers"

This same Elijah the prophet appeared in the dispensation of the fullness of times in the Kirtland Temple on April 3, 1836 to the Prophet Joseph Smith (Doctrine & Covenants 110:13–16). He restored the keys of the sealing power of the priesthood to Joseph and began planting in the hearts of the children the promises made to the fathers. With that seed, the hearts of the children began to turn to their fathers. (Doctrine & Covenants 2). The need to belong to the Family Tree of Man became important and with turning hearts, descendants began looking for their ancestors.

The following year, in 1837, the Registrar General of Births, Marriages, and Deaths set up office in Somerset House, England. The office gave the public access to records in ways never before possible. To some, the timing might seem to be coincidental. Others see it as opening the door for the fulfillment of Elijah's prophecy. Help started flowing from both sides of the veil as people the world over began a passionate quest for their roots.

Members of The Church of Jesus Christ of Latter-day Saints treasure these and other family-history records because we believe the turning of hearts is happening for a unique purpose—that of ensuring families are united eternally through work performed in temples (Doctrine & Covenants Section 124: 29–55). This work includes baptism and other ordinances such as the sealing—or binding—of a husband and wife in marriage for eternity instead of for this life only and the sealing of their children to them as a family. Freedom to choose is, and always will be, a vital part of the Savior's gospel, both in this life and the next. Ancestors can accept or reject temple work completed on their behalf.

Discovering my ancestors intrigues me and draws me to look to the past for understanding and direction today. I often wonder, when a looming accident of some sort is averted, whether ancestors are the angels watching out for me because they love me and know I'm working to connect our family tree.

Unraveling mysteries is satisfying. At one time, I could not find one family on my father's side. According to my dad, his father's father (my great-grandfather), Alfred Tozer, born 1844, London, England, had seven children. I found details for six, but despite much searching, clues about Alfred and Sarah's daughter Lillie Tozer did not seem to exist. I knew she was born in Soho, London, England, in the late 1800s, but not one descendant of the other six children had further information. Lillie's name lodged in my mind, but I didn't know where else to explore.

Then one Sunday evening in 1986, when we still lived in England, I received a phone call from a lady whose maiden name was Winifred Strange.

Winifred had been listening to Charlie Chester's interactive radio program, *Sunday Soapbox*, and called Charlie to say she was looking for anyone who knew anything about her mother's family, as she had no idea who her relatives or ancestors were. She gave her mother's maiden name as Lillie Tozer, born 1885, Soho, London, England.

At that same moment, a distant relative named Derek Styles, who lived in Norfolk, England, happened to be listening to the program. I had corresponded with Derek years before about my great-great-grandmother, Emma Scarfe, born 1823 in Redgrave-cum-Botesdale, Suffolk, who married Robert John Whall. Emma's daughter, Sarah Ann Whall, who was born in 1849, married Alfred Tozer—Lillie's father. When Derek heard Winifred's request, he remembered the Tozer name, called the radio host, and gave my name and number.

An excited Winifred immediately called, and we shared information that filled gaps for both of us. Then came the fun part. When Winifred married, her surname became Collins. She also decided to change her first name to June. They named one of their boys Phil, now famous around the globe for his musical talent, selling millions of albums worldwide. Their other son, Clive, is also world renowned for his award-winning artistic skills creating cartoons for top magazines and newspapers. Their daughter, Carole, made a name for herself with her skating achievements.

Such famous people might not hide among your branches, but learning where you came from and to whom you belong is exciting, no matter what you discover. I hope this book inspires you to hunt for your kindred dead and find those missing links. I believe ancestors often decide to help. We just need to reach out and receive the connections.

There's a Couple Named Jollow Around the Corner

Sherry Ann Miller, Author—Washington, USA

In 1997, I had a den full of bulging files filled with ancestral history and tidbits gathered over the previous eleven years. I was writing a family history on my mother's maternal line, *The David and Martha (Haws) Timothy History*. Having just completed this massive work, I thought I'd now like to start on Mama's paternal line.

However, as I walked into my den early one morning, I heard a woman's voice speak to me as clearly as if she were standing right beside me. Her simple words: "Sherry Ann, you have enough information in this den to find my family." Amazingly, I recognized the woman as my great-grandmother Mary Ann Jollow Stone (born December 1862, Liskeard, Cornwall, England, raised in Llantrisant, Glamorgan, Wales), who died shortly before my fourth birthday. Mary Ann is my father's grandmother on his paternal side.

I glanced around my den in dismay. Everywhere I looked, I saw folders and files containing thousands of names, mostly on my mother's lines. I had one sparse little file on Jollow. I didn't know what Great-grandmother saw in my den that I couldn't see. Noticing my chair in front of my desk, my eyes were suddenly riveted on the computer screen. If there was anything in my den that might help me find my great-grandmother's Jollow line, it had to be the computer.

Eagerly, I sat down, ready to begin. As I pondered how the computer could help me, it popped into my mind that someone who carried the surname *Jollow* might still be living in the village in Wales where Mary Ann grew up. Immediately, I went to www.rootsweb.com and signed up for the forum on Glamorgan, Wales.

I wrote to the forum, stating, "I am looking for anyone by the name of Jollow living in or near the town of Llantrisant in Glamorgan, Wales," and left my contact information

Half an hour later, I received an email from a woman who wrote, "There is a couple around the corner from me in Llantrisant whose surname is Jollow. Give me your contact information, and I will see if they're interested in making your acquaintance."

I wrote back, "I am the great-granddaughter of Mary Ann Jollow, whose parents, Richard Jollow and Ann Gill, settled in Llantrisant about 1870. Mary Ann Jollow married Charles Stone and migrated with him and their family to the USA about 1899."

I recorded my address and phone number, and sent the email off with a prayer in my heart that the Jollow couple living in Llantrisant might somehow connect to Mary Ann.

As I was preparing the noon meal for my husband that day, I was excited to tell him about the morning's experiences. He was taking off his boots when the telephone rang. To my great surprise, it was a woman named Dianne Jollow, married to a Ray Jollow, calling from Llantrisant, Glamorgan, Wales. For many years, they'd tried to find out what happened to Mary Ann Jollow. Some of the family thought she died young, but others thought she married and moved to America.

Ray and Dianne were thrilled to learn what happened to Mary Ann, and by the end of our lengthy conversation, we shared postal addresses, as they had no computer, and agreed to exchange information.

I served lunch with tear-filled eyes, amazed at how quickly I'd found Mary Ann's family with the use of the Internet in my little den. Great-grandmother was right. That very afternoon, I prepared family group sheets and family history stories in a booklet and mailed them to Ray and Dianne Jollow in Llantrisant.

A week or two later, I received a package from the Jollows of Llantrisant. In it, I found information on all of Mary Ann's siblings and their descendants, as well as information about her ancestors five generations back from Mary Ann, documented in an orderly manner, including photocopies of sources.

To make this delightful event sweeter, a year later Ray and Dianne Jollow took a trip to San Diego, where I met them with my aunt and uncle (Ray and Uncle are second cousins). Surprisingly, we learned that about ten years earlier, my uncle and aunt had toured Llantrisant and taken photos of the house Mary Ann's father built, not knowing that Ray and Dianne lived in that very house. Had they thought to knock on the door, we would have found the Jollow information years earlier.

Thank goodness I had learned to listen by the time Mary Ann spoke to me in my little den that morning. A few years after Ray and Diane's visit to San Diego, Ray died.

Filling the Gap—with Precision

John Counsel, Business Consultant/Trainer/Author—Australia

I want to express my profound gratitude to my sister, Marg Counsel, for her unflagging dedication and consistent efforts in tracing our family history. I stand in awe of her achievements, and want to go on public record in declaring my love, admiration and gratitude for and to her. I'm humble and grateful to be her brother.

Marg and I have plenty of great stories of miraculous events in family-history research that now dates back to the 900s on one line and 1061 on another (earliest known uses of the *Counsel* surname). One story is about the miraculous closing of a five-hundred-year gap on one line after my sister discovered a missing family branch and decided to visit them in Vancouver, BC, on her way from our home in Australia to the UK for a year of family-history research.

On her first night in Canada, my sister laid out the research on either side of the gap for her newfound relatives. The husband wandered off for a while, then returned with an ancient family Bible with a long list of names and dates. It started with the name of the last person on the early side of the gap that we had traced, and ended with the first person on our side of the five-hundred-year gap. Problem solved!

We had spent almost thirty fruitless years on these lines until my father died. The day before he passed over, my mother told him that he needed to help us out from the other side of the veil.

Since my father's death, the information has been almost overwhelming, and the incidents surrounding them are nothing short of thrilling. Two more of our stories appear in this book on pages sixty-five and seventy.

In the Right Place at the Right Time

Sarah Street Hinze, B.S., Author, Speaker, Educator, Therapist—
Arizona, USA

Many years ago I awoke in the early morning with a thought I knew came from the Lord. "Sarah, if you will arise early today and read your scriptures, the Lord will give you a gift."

I followed the prompting, read the scriptures, and said my prayers. I began my morning activities in anticipation of receiving guidance from the Spirit, and soon I received a strong feeling that I should visit my parents in Tennessee.

We were living in Utah at the time. I had seen my parents only a year earlier, but to follow the prompting, I called the travel agency anyway. I explained to the agent that I wanted round trip airfare but had a limited amount of money. I asked her if she could find a discounted airplane ticket. She laughed. To meet my request, she would have to find something less than half the regular price.

"I really don't think anything like that is available," she said, "but I'll check the computer."

All day long I awaited her call. Finally, that evening, the phone rang.

"I don't know how this happened," she exclaimed, "but there are a few tickets available for the price you quoted me."

I was able to make the trip to Tennessee. My parents and I had a joyous reunion, but after a few days, I began to wonder and prayed, "Lord, what is my purpose here?"

I explained my feelings to my mother, who was a not a member of The Church of Jesus Christ of Latter-day Saints at the time. She told me about a woman whom she had met at the beauty shop a few weeks earlier. The woman's married name was Street—my maiden name—and her husband had done extensive research on the Street family line.

I went to visit Clay and Martha Street. They met me with gentle graciousness and Southern hospitality. Clay showed me his books of family history, and I learned that we had the same Street family line. He gave me vital information about more than one hundred of our common ancestors. All of the dates necessary for me to perform their temple work had been carefully documented.

I was amazed as Clay, who was not a member of the LDS Church, shared with me his desire to search out his family line. He told me of an experience he had that was similar to my own. One day he felt impressed to drive sixty miles to North Carolina to visit his aunt. There he copied many of the names and information he found in the little local family cemetery. He suspected that some of the information dated back one hundred and thirty years, and that the cemetery was the only known source for the birth and death dates of some of these ancestors. When he arrived at his aunt's house that evening, he prepared his materials so he could return to the cemetery early the next morning.

That night, heavy rain began to fall, and Clay could not sleep. He became more and more anxious to get back to the cemetery. Finally, tired of fighting his feelings, he jumped out of bed, threw on his aunt's raincoat and rain boots, grabbed her umbrella, and headed for the cemetery.

Using a flashlight, Clay guided his way through the downpour to the tombstones and copied down the names and dates he needed. Feeling satisfied, he returned to his aunt's house and slept through the night.

The next morning, he arose to a beautiful sunrise. The rainclouds were gone. Clay decided to drive over to the cemetery again and take one more look around. When he arrived at the cemetery, bulldozers were there. A house was under construction nearby, and, without knowing it, the bulldozer operators were pushing dirt onto the little cemetery, covering it. He then understood why he'd felt such a strong desire to go there the night before.

He let me copy all of the information he had on our related genealogy.

As I left the Streets' house to find a copy machine, Clay advised me to go to the one in the university library a few blocks away. I felt prompted to honor his request. I went to the university and copied all the materials. As I was paying the librarian, she said, "Oh, it looks like you are doing genealogy. What line are you working on?"

"Well, this is the Street line," I explained. "But the line I really need is the Garland line from Carter County, Tennessee."

"Did you say 'the Garland line from Carter County'?" she asked.

"Yes," I answered, somewhat startled.

"There is a lady in the back room who is president of the Garland Family Research Club. Her main lines run out of Carter County, Tennessee," she said.

After talking to the woman in the back room, I left with information on more than one hundred more of my ancestors—with everything documented and verified.

This all happened in one afternoon. I was thrilled and humbled at this great gift the Lord had given me. My husband and I, with the help of friends and family, eventually were able to do the temple work for more than two hundred of my ancestors.

I learned to my amazement that my Garland line had organized a Garland Family Research Association and met yearly. A few years later, I attended their meeting in North Carolina and met a distant uncle, Paul Garland. Paul's parents had been baptized in North Carolina by Apostle Charles Callis many years before.

Paul told me of his father taking him around to meet the relatives and collect their genealogy. He informed me that before his father died, he'd instructed Paul to continue gathering the names and then to send them to the temple so their work could be done. Since Paul was not active in the LDS Church, he handed me copies of his entire research, bound in two hardback books, and said, "Sarah, I have done the research, and now I am asking you to do the temple work for our ancestors."

This experience has been one of the highlights of my life. I know that many of my ancestors were ready and eager to have their temple work done. I felt them near me as I was doing their work. I had many sacred experiences in the temple, and doing the work for my ancestors brought a rich renewal of my faith in the power of the Lord. I am grateful to my Uncle Paul Garland and for Clay Street for the spirit of Elijah they carried with them to complete the research on our family and for the honor of doing their work in the holy temples.

Learning that Genealogy is more than just Names and Dates

Daris Howard, Author, Playwright, Math professor—BYU Idaho, USA

My foray into genealogy didn't start in the way it usually begins with most people—that is, wanting to find out dates and places about ancestors. I really didn't feel a need. I had aunts who had done that back to Adam and Eve and even beyond, or at least I thought so. That was a good excuse, because my life was busy, and I had absolutely no desire to make it busier.

But I learned that family history deals with a lot more than knowing the births, deaths, marriages, and other important dates and places for those who preceded us. It has to do with their lives, their dreams and hopes, their aspirations, and how those things have, in turn, made each of us what we are.

My initiation came in a very small and seemingly insignificant way. I was sitting in a priesthood leadership meeting when the president of our stake asked us to think of things we could do, a couple of years in the future, to celebrate the sesquicentennial of the arrival of the Church's first wagon train in Utah. Out of nowhere came the thought that I should write a musical.

I smiled to myself, wondering where such an odd idea came from. Though I wrote stories for my children, and even wrote a song or two now and then, I had never done anything for anyone outside my family, and definitely nothing of that magnitude.

I went back to listening to our stake president, and the thought came again. I considered the fact that my knowledge of plays came from watching them. I had never been in any kind of production since grade school. I didn't know how to write a play. I told myself the thought was absolutely crazy and tried to push it from my mind. But the harder I tried to get rid of it, the more often, and stronger, it came.

Every morning when I woke up, and every time my mind was free, thoughts about the musical would interject themselves. I continued to laugh at the idea, saying it was impossible to do with my lack of theater experience.

Shortly thereafter, I received a call from a lady in my stake asking me to audition for the part of Jud in the musical *Oklahoma*. I thought the invitation coming on the heels of my musical thoughts was nothing but a strange coincidence, and told her I was too busy. She then called my wife and asked her to convince me to try out. My wife, Donna, knowing of the insights I'd been having, agreed to encourage me.

We were on our way to go camping when Donna asked me to pull into the church parking lot.

"Why?" I asked.

"Oh, just for something."

I pulled our van in, towing the big camper behind us. When we came to a stop, she said, "I think you should go in and just do the reading for the part in the musical."

I told her I didn't want to and almost started driving again, but she reminded me of the impressions and convinced me that the audition wouldn't take long. I felt the same feeling come again, telling me I should do this, and that feeling, along with Donna's urging, convinced me to finally go in for the reading. When I stepped into the room, I met someone who desperately wanted the part of Jud. We both read for it, as well as for a few others, and as I was leaving, I told the director she should give the part to the other person because I was way too busy.

While we were camping I told Donna that Jud didn't seem like a fun part anyway. I made the mistake of saying that the character of Ali Hackim, the peddler, would be more enjoyable to play.

Thinking I'd put the whole thing behind me, I was surprised a few days later to find that the director had called to ask if I would mind taking the part of Ali Hackim. Donna, believing I wanted the part, accepted on my behalf, telling the director I said it would be a better part anyway.

I was flabbergasted. "I didn't say I *wanted* to do it," I said. "I just mentioned that part would be more fun!"

With lots of encouragement and a few more promptings, I ended up doing it. During the whole summer of practice, I didn't feel any more impressions about writing a musical, so I figured I had completed what was desired of me. But the minute the musical ended, the promptings returned, with a different slant. Now it was as if someone was telling me that my claim of never having been in a musical was no longer an excuse. *Being in one musical does not make a person a playwright,* I thought, and again ignored the feelings.

Then, one day, later in the summer, Donna and our seven children were in an automobile accident. I spent many quiet, anxious hours in the hospital. They all recovered completely, but during those long, contemplative hours, the promptings came to be almost overwhelming. I could hardly sleep, and anytime I woke up, the prompting was immediately there.

One day, after everyone was home and recovered, I left at five in the morning to go to the temple. As I drove through a long, narrow valley, with the sun shining behind the mountains to the east, another impression came with great force. Someone asked me, "What do I have to do to get your attention on this?"

With a feeling of exasperation, I spoke aloud as I drove. "All right. What am I supposed to write a musical about?" I no sooner said it than thoughts and ideas flooded my mind. I immediately knew it was to be a musical about my ancestors. That was extremely clear. Outlines for a story filled my head.

Later that evening, I holed up in my office and started typing. I placed a tape recorder nearby. As I wrote, ideas for songs came into my mind—sometimes with lyrics, sometimes just the music—and I recorded them on the tape recorder.

I told Donna to go to bed, and I continued to work into the night. By the time I went to bed, I had the whole musical outlined, together with some fifteen songs.

The next month and a half were a whirlwind of activity as I typed as fast as I could every free minute. I purchased music software, and Donna, always supportive, transcribed the songs from the cassette tape into the computer. As soon as I thought about a new scene, ideas and dialogue flooded into my mind.

I told Donna, "It's as if someone is standing at my shoulder speaking to me."

There were times I also felt as if someone said, "No. You erase that scene and start over." If I balked at redoing my work, I felt more promptings and had more sleepless nights until I finally did it right. I felt especially influenced to create a certain song for one very touching point in the musical, but every time I tried to sit down and write lyrics, they always felt wrong. Finally, I received a strong impression to wait—the time would come.

As I continued working, I kept thinking I should take some time and read the family histories. I had only a vague sense about anything to do with my ancestors, because I'd never been interested. I didn't even know their names, and yet here I was, supposedly writing their story. Whenever I came to a point in the musical where I needed a name, I put in whatever came to mind to keep the story moving forward, because ideas were coming too fast to stop. I resolved to go back later when I had time to look up any available information.

The fall arrived, and with it came Thanksgiving. My brother invited us to his house for dinner. He was an avid family-history buff, and owned almost every available book about the family. Normally, I sat around and visited, but this particular year I ended up with a raging headache.

I asked my brother if I might take one of the family books and go lie down. As I read, something unexpected happened. The names I thought I'd made up for the musical were in the book. Stories I thought I'd created for the sake of the musical were in the book. I knew I'd never heard the stories before, never knew the people's names, and yet there they were in front of me. The record was brief, in journal form, but their stories had come into my mind vibrant and full of detail.

I suddenly felt a humility I'd never experienced before—and a sorrow for the way I'd fought against doing this work, needing such pressure to start it. In addition, I felt humble I'd been chosen, and repentant for arrogantly beginning to think the work was my own. With renewed dedication, I vowed to keep working.

As Christmas approached, everything was finished with the exception of the one song. I again tried to write lyrics for it, but everything seemed empty. The song was supposed to be for a mother singing to her dying child, but nothing I tried carried the depth of feeling I knew it needed.

Then, on December 23rd, our own baby was delivered—stillborn. As Donna and I were alone in the hospital room, the overwhelming loss of this little one for whom we had planned and prepared and loved even before her birth, filled our aching hearts. I could hardly breathe from the pain I felt while driving away, leaving Donna to recover in the hospital room.

When I reached home and told the children, we all felt a great loss. As soon as they were in bed, I went into my room and fell on my knees, sobbing my heart out to my Heavenly Father. As I did, I suddenly felt as if someone put a hand on my shoulder and said, "Now is the time to write the song." I went to my office and wrote the lyrics, which this time not only felt inspired, but which I now experienced deep within my heart.

The lyrics needed minimal adjustment to fit the music, in contrast to the other songs, which needed far more revision to work. I suppose, in order to write that song, I needed to feel what my ancestors had felt when burying children on cold, desolate plains so many years ago.

Once the musical, *Lilacs in the Valley* was complete (see http://www.dramasource.com/itempage.php?script=ALIAB for the full musical), we wondered if there would be a chance to perform it.

The next summer during the sesquicentennial, we worked with an experienced director to help me put the production together. The whole time we were practicing and producing, I felt as if unseen people stood by me. However, three major events especially deserve telling.

At one point, the choreographer wanted one of the characters do a modern disco-type dance. As distinctly as anything I'd heard, it seemed as if someone spoke to me saying, "Don't you dare let her do that to me!" Although the choreographer was adamant we do it, I persevered, and the dance was changed. I had the distinct feeling the person involved was giving me thanks.

Another time, while rehearsing the end of the musical, I felt it didn't have the closure I knew it needed. The family had lost so many members they loved, and even though there was an underlying theme of families being together again after this life, it didn't portray that emphasis to the extent I wanted.

Then I had the strong prompting to put the family members who had died back into a final scene. I conferred with my co-director. He said it was a bad idea and tried to talk me out of it. I suggested we attempt it anyway, because I felt impressed to do it. We couldn't try until the next night after arranging for the right costuming and getting everything in place. We told no one except the necessary actors what we were going to do, so when the time came, the rest of the cast sat in the audience.

When the scene played out, the auditorium was absolutely still. The new power of that scene brought together what the whole musical was trying to say, and did it without another single word being added. At the end, the other director turned to me and with great emotion said, "I don't know how you've got your ideas throughout this musical, but I promise I won't question them again."

As the curtain closed to a standing ovation on the last night, I felt moved to find a quiet place alone. I found a room, and in the solitude, it seemed as if someone once more spoke to my mind saying, "We are leaving you now. We're proud of you."

In my heart, I told them I didn't want them to leave, but the feeling came that there were other things they needed to do. Once more, it seemed as if someone put a hand on my shoulder and spoke. "You've done a good job on this. Now continue writing, but be sure to only write things we can all be proud of." With that, the feeling someone was standing with me gradually faded over the course of about ten minutes. It was almost as if each individual hugged me before leaving.

I've never again encountered the same feelings I had through that whole experience. I grew to know family members who preceded me in ways I could never have imagined. Words cannot fully express the effect they had on me. At times, I knew their personalities and captured them in small ways in the story's characters. I felt as if they laughed with me and sometimes cried with me.

But the most important thing I learned was that they are real people, not just names in a book or lists on a genealogy sheet.

Jane

David P. Vandagriff, Attorney/Author—Utah, USA

My ancestor, Jane Bane Weir, moved with her family from Virginia to Pilot Grove, Iowa, about 25 miles from Nauvoo, in 1851. Unlike towns along the Mississippi River, Pilot Grove was and is tiny, more of an idea than a community. Shortly after the family arrived, Jane's husband, Major John Ringland, died of cholera, leaving her to raise four children alone.

Jane supported her family by teaching school. Her children remembered being awakened on pitch-dark winter mornings when they were small and traveling with their mother to school, some sitting in front of her and some behind on the family's only horse.

The school was often icy-cold when they arrived. The children helped their mother start a fire in the stove, bring in enough wood for the day, break the ice on the water barrel, draw more water to refill the barrel, and perform every other task necessary to make the school ready for the arrival of the other students. At the end of the school day, Jane's children helped her clean the school and prepare it for the next morning then everyone remounted the horse and rode home in the dark. At home, Jane began her second arduous job: keeping house and caring for her children's physical, emotional, and spiritual needs.

The early lessons, both academic and spiritual, that Jane taught in her humble home and small country schoolhouse bore rich fruit. One of her sons obtained his doctorate of divinity degree and became the minister of a large church in St. Louis. Another son became a medical doctor, specializing in the treatment of tuberculosis, before he turned to the ministry during his middle years and served a congregation in Oklahoma City. A third son was a prosperous Iowa farmer and the presiding elder in his local church. Due to the rigors of her early years, Jane became an invalid as she aged, and her only daughter cared for Jane until her death.

I was fortunate to locate some of the words preached by her sons at her funeral, together with written memorials, one jointly prepared by her children and another by a friend. From them, a picture of Jane's legacy becomes clear:

> Never for one day did she lose courage in those trying times. Out of the bleak surroundings as out of more prosperous ones, she firmly held to the faith that God doeth all things well. She was descended from generations of cultivated people, and under all conditions and at all times there was a certain aristocratic bearing which made one remember just who she was and from whence she came.

> Our mother was all that could be desired. Intellectually strong, affectionately kind, always ambitious for the best things, courageous, cheerful, a good student of the world progress, a lover of children and beloved by them.

> A Christian mother is a great deep of ponderings, a charm of sacrifices, a perpetual prayer, a medley of hopes and fears, an illuminating example. She is sent of God to illustrate the meaning of the words, 'This is the way, walk ye in it.'

> God made mothers before he made ministers. Such is a faithful mother's reward to live on in the lives and services of her children. By the side of such a mother, the life of a man is small.

> She left no great heritage of gold, but to her children she left a better legacy, the memory of a faith that never failed, a courage that never faltered, a life triumphant.

During the process of gathering the material that told Jane's story, both my wife and I gained a vivid sense of this truly amazing woman. Jane spent her life in tiny places, performing great works before small audiences—her children and the few people who lived near her.

We learned about Jane while we were living in Missouri in 1989. Our closest temple was in Dallas, about seven hours away. My wife and I traveled to Texas one weekend to visit.

When we entered the sealing room, we didn't know any of the other people who would assist us with our family names. The sealer asked us each to introduce ourselves. Most patrons were from the Dallas area, but one young couple traveled from Louisiana. The session began, and from time to time, the temple sealer rotated the couples acting as proxies and the witnesses. We were performing sealings for a number of my ancestors, and I was enjoying a calm and peaceful spirit.

The couple from Louisiana were acting as proxies for the husbands and wives when the temple sealer spoke Jane's name. The wife immediately began to weep, and a powerful wave of pure joy swept through the room. Everyone, including the sealer, wept, and the work had to stop for several minutes midway through Jane's sealing, until everyone could bring strong emotions back under control.

No one in the room besides me and my wife had any idea who Jane was before that moment. Each of us received a spiritual introduction to that remarkable woman and felt her joy at reuniting with a beloved husband after so many years.

The sealer began the sealing of Jane to John again, speaking slowly. The emotions in the room were still very intense, but Jane restrained her joyous spirit long enough for her sealing to be completed.

After the session, the sealer asked my wife and me to remain in the sealing room after the others left. He asked about what happened, and we told him Jane's story. The sealer then looked at me and said, "In addition to being a temple sealer, I am also a patriarch. I want you to know that the reason you were born into your family was to do the work you performed today in the temple."

"The worth of souls is great in the sight of God." (Doctrine and Covenants 18:10) Jane was born more than 120 years before I was. The worth of this one single woman was so great that the Lord sent me into her family then led me to the Church so I could receive the missionary lessons, be baptized and endowed and take her name to the temple, where sacred ordinances could permanently unite her with her husband, children and parents.

Elder Merrill J. Bateman has said:

> For many years I thought of the Savior's experience in the garden and on the cross as places where a large mass of sin was heaped upon Him. Through the words of Alma, Abinadi, Isaiah, and other prophets, however, my view has changed. Instead of an impersonal mass of sin, there was a long line of people, as Jesus felt 'our infirmities' (Hebrews 4:15), "[bore] our griefs . . . carried our sorrows . . . [and] was bruised for our iniquities.' (Isaiah 53:4–5)

> The Atonement was an intimate, personal experience in which Jesus came to know how to help each of us. (Merrill J. Bateman, "A Pattern for All," *Ensign*, Nov 2005, 74)

The Savior knows Jane. He knew her before she was born. While she was living on the earth, He heard every prayer, counted every tear, understood every worry, and felt every pain of her spirit and body. Through His marvelous Atonement, Jesus saved Jane, together with her husband and children. He has removed every sorrow she ever felt and replaced it with pure, powerful, and eternal joy.

Finding the McRae Family

Adapted from the journal of Wilda Wimmer McRae (1908–1998).
Wilda was a Swing-Shift Lead Welder for McDonnell Douglas
Aircraft, USA, in the 1960s.

On one particular day as my husband Jerry and I searched for our
ancestors, we knew our Father in Heaven was helping us.

After seeing the old house where Jerry's mother, Beulah Tozier
McRae, lived, and the old cemeteries at Thrasher and Mount Olivet
near where Jerry went to church and school, we went to Palmyra
Missouri, Marion County, and with mounting excitement searched
land records, marriage records, and old wills.

In the land records, we found a grant given to Jerry's great-great-
grandfather William McRae for the land where the Old Basket Farm is
now located. John Quincy Adams, President of the United States, had
signed and sealed the document.

Then Jerry went through the marriage records and found an entry for
James Franklin McRae and Ellen Huskey, which meant that his great-
great-grandfather was not named just Frank McRae as we had always
supposed, but *James Franklin* McRae. This explained why we couldn't
find him in other records. Jerry was so excited that from then on, he no
longer complained about how much money I spent on research.

Next, we got into wills, and that was even more exciting. We found
James Franklin McRae's will and could hardly wait to go outside and
read it. However, the beautiful writing was too small to decipher. He
had listed many people and included their birth dates, for which I
blessed him, thinking they were names and dates of his children's
births.

We crossed the street and bought a magnifying glass to read the will. It turned out that James Franklin McRae had named his children, all right, but the names with birthdates were for his slaves. He had nineteen slaves—thirteen women and six men. We were not too excited about that until we read that he divided the slaves among his children, and said that if they tried to sell the slaves or give them away, the slaves would be freed automatically. He also said that on reaching the age of forty, each slave would be released from bondage.

The will went to probate about 1848, some twenty years before the abolition of slavery, so I think of James Franklin McRae as a kind and compassionate man.

We then went to Shelbina to see if we could find anything about the half brother of my husband's father (Ora Granville McRae), Roma McRae.

It was after five when we arrived, so Jerry suggested I visit the courthouse while he went to the mortuary. I soon discovered that everyone except the district judge had gone home. However, when I told the judge we couldn't come back because we had to be in St. Louis the next day, he got out the book of marriages and showed me how to use it. He was so nice and didn't seem to mind helping me, even though the courthouse was officially closed.

I could not find the marriage record of Roma, so I thanked him and went back to the car. Jerry said the mortuary was also closed, but when he descended the stairs, he noticed a little old man standing there, so asked him if he had ever heard of Roma McRae.

The old man said, "I sure did. I worked with him for twenty years."

Of all the people in the world, Roma's coworker just happened to be standing on that sidewalk at that moment. He said he knew of a man who lived next door to where Roma and his mother used to live and told us how to get there.

When we arrived, the man invited us in, and after a long visit, he took us to the cemetery and showed us Roma's grave. It had a double tombstone with Roma's name and dates on one side and his wife's name and dates on the other.

These experiences increased my testimony that when we are doing the Lord's work, he is right there to help us.

Family History Brings Happy Closure
Wendy Hendry—Utah, USA

I found my birth mom, Jan, about two years ago. She is not a member of The Church of Jesus Christ of Latter-day Saints, but when I was born, she insisted an LDS family adopt me because she respected the Church's family values and wanted me raised in a good home.

When Jan and I finally met, we bonded right away. But even before that, I had the strong feeling I needed to do her family history work, especially on her mother's side of the family.

My birth mom was happy for me to work on her history but didn't see any need for urgency. She'd kept her pregnancy a secret from her parents, my grandparents, when they were alive, so they never knew I existed. When I asked if she would call some of the older relatives to ask for help filling out pedigree charts, Jan was hesitant to talk with them.

One Sunday, while researching my grandmother's family in the family history center at Brigham Young University, I began to pray fervently for help. I specifically prayed Jan would receive a desire to help me find the information I needed.

The next day, Monday, I received a call from Jan saying she had the strangest experience on Sunday night when lying in bed. She told me she was not a spiritual person, but she couldn't deny what she was about to tell me. She said her mother appeared and sat on the bed with her back against the headboard as she often did when Jan was young. Her mom said how happy she and Jan's father were that Jan found me after all these years, adding how much they liked me, and that everything I was doing with family history was good. Jan said she'd never seen her mother looking so happy.

After Jan related this to me, she immediately wanted to contact all her relatives to find as much information as possible. I was able to go to the temple to do the work for my grandparents and each of their parents. It was such a wonderful experience.

I've often thought it amazing that I was asked to be a family history consultant at church the year before this happened. Before that, I didn't know anything about genealogy, but because I accepted the call and learned how to research, I was prepared when the opportunity came to unite my birth mother's family.

Portals to the Past

Donna Mason Hamm—Colorado, USA

My father, John William Mason, drowned when I was two. Before that, my parents divorced and both remarried. What followed for me was years of fractured family life too painful to share. I didn't know anything about my dad or extended family, and didn't feel as though I truly belonged to anyone. What I now know about my family history is the result of an amazing journey on which I'm convinced I've been led by ancestors. And I'm sure Dad has been right there with them, guiding me.

 I grew up with a great curiosity about my daddy and the love I was sure he had for me, but I could find no answers about him or his past. To make matters more difficult, my mom remarried a man in the Air Force, which began many years of travelling around the country, living in various locations. Later, I, too married an Airman, and my travels continued. I was fully disconnected from my Mason roots.

When my husband and I finally decided to settle in Colorado, I never dreamed I'd come full-circle, back to where my Irish Mason family started out in America. And I never dreamed I would find a connection between my Mason family and the Gunnison Diversion Tunnel—something I discovered the same day my grandson Mason Liam was born. I can imagine conversations taking place in the spirit world that day as events unfolded, filled with Mason links, both past and present—links proving I belong to a wonderful family.

To backtrack a little—a few years ago, I received an email saying, "My name is John William Mason." My daddy's name! I nearly fainted. The email explained he was the son of my daddy's brother and was named after my father. His dad was in the boat when they found my daddy's body. This was incredible for me. I had an actual living family member, and he wanted to find me. Not only that, but he gathered every available piece of Mason-related information to share with me. And so my fascination with genealogy began.

In the spring of 2009, my husband and I were travelling in Colorado for a few days' break and spent the night in Montrose so we could revisit Black Canyon in Gunnison National Park. One thing I knew about Montrose was that my Mason family once lived close by. They were listed on the 1910 census as living in River Portal—a place I hadn't been able to locate.

The next morning as we entered the park, I noticed a sign off to the right of the road, just before the ranger station: East Portal Road. I felt goose bumps. "Portal" plus "Montrose" equaled possibilities. Still . . . it was a long shot and probably had nothing to do with River Portal. We went to the Visitors' Center and they were showing a film. Somewhere during the movie, I heard the magic words "River Portal." The hairs on my whole body stood on end.

The movie talked about Irish and Italian immigrants who helped build a tunnel to divert the Gunnison River. I could not believe my ears. Because of things my cousin John had told me, I knew our great-grandfather, John Patrick Mason, had been a miner. I had a picture of him in front of a tunnel entrance, standing among a group of miners (third from the left—behind the man in the suit with the paper & pen). And although I really tried, I never was able to identify that tunnel or the mine.

Then the film showed a miner in an unusual hat. The only time I ever saw such a hat before was in the picture of my great-grandfather at the tunnel entrance.

Sitting through the rest of that movie was difficult. Every cell in me was screaming, "I've found River Portal. I've found the connection to my family."

The minute the movie ended, I rushed out to the woman behind the counter and asked if she had a list of people who had worked on the tunnel. As I told them about my family and my thoughts during the movie, I could see their attention growing. Then they told me. 2009 was the hundredth anniversary of the Gunnison Diversion Tunnel. In honor of the centennial celebrations, park rangers had documented the history of the tunnel, but they didn't know much about the people who'd lived there.

These women also told me River Portal no longer existed, but remains of it were down at the bottom of the gorge—down East Portal Road, the place I'd seen the sign for at the entrance.

So we braved the trip down and sat a moment next to the Gunnison River. There wasn't much to see apart from a little old house with a neat garden, nothing to show that a small town ever existed. I felt something though. I *knew* my family had been there. Not nearby—but right *there*. I knew it.

A man appeared outside the house, so I asked him if he could tell me where the remains of River Portal were. He said, "You're standing on them." He then told us his house was the only one remaining from that time and that he worked for the water company that controlled the dam. It turned out he and his wife had begun work on their genealogy over the winter, and that very morning had made a huge discovery about their own family. I knew then, that this man understood my quest.

I asked where the tunnel was, because I couldn't see any sign of it. He replied, "Let me get the key." Can you imagine? He had the key. And he was going to show me the tunnel. Jerry led my husband and me to a place we never would have imagined. I felt such a mixture of emotions as we walked through a fence into a little building. I saw nothing resembling a tunnel entrance, and yet there were those goose bumps again. Jerry explained that the little building was there to hide the entrance. Ahead of us was pitch dark. And then I heard the sound of water lapping.

Tears ran down my face. I felt surrounded by friendly spirits. It was a warm, comforting, beautiful experience. A thought jumped into my head: *The ancestors are smiling.* I knew I'd found *the* tunnel. We walked into the darkness and found a portal to the past.

When we got home, I was eager to document my findings. I didn't need documentation, but I'm a genealogist, and documentation is important to us. I checked the 1910 census again. How could I have missed or forgotten what I'd found there before? I'd been doing research for years. It's not like me to miss an important piece of information. Yet there it was, right there on the census: my great-grandfather's occupation—*driller*, and his place of employment—

tunnel. Confirmation! I had the documentation I needed to prove my connection to River Portal was exactly what I'd come to believe. I felt incredibly proud of my great-grandfather.

I later found out more information from the Tunnel park rangers. It seems there were three known pictures of that group of miners at the tunnel entrance. One was in the National Archives. The second was in the Denver archives, and the third belonged to the water company involved with the project. They had no idea a fourth picture (mine) sexisted. But they confirmed it was definitely the right tunnel. In my search for a tunnel and a mine, I'd looked for mineral mines, and never thought of looking for anything to do with water.

I learned something else extraordinary. The park selected that tunnel entrance photo as the cover for the brochure related to the centennial celebrations, and they selected it before they knew a thing about my family connections or me. There were an unusual number of pictures taken at River Portal, no doubt due to the precedent-setting nature of the project. There must have been many photographs to choose from. Yet they chose the one I knew was mine. Amazing!

Spunky William

Elizabeth Jane Roberts, Researcher and Educator—Gloucestershire, England

For many years, I tried to find more information about my maternal 4th great-grandfather, William Gaze. His surname was often misspelled and hard to track down. After forty years, I finally found his marriage to Mary Ann in the town of Stogumber in Somerset. Unfortunately, since the period was before general registration, I found no information about William's father.

William continued to baffle me. I couldn't find him on the censuses, and he wasn't living with his family. I'd heard he was in service as a butler, so tried to find suitable big houses that might have a record of him, to no avail. Two of his children's marriage certificates mentioned him; one said he was deceased and the other, earlier, marriage certificate didn't mention his death, so I surmised he died at some point between the two.

I have the habit of talking aloud to my ancestors at times. Of course, one-sided conversations are the norm. "William," I said one day, as I realized I'd run out of ideas and patience. "I can't connect you to your parents if I don't know where you were born! You must tell me where to find your record. Who were your parents?"

I was shocked to receive a sure and reasoned response. "You find all my grandchildren and great-grandchildren, and then I will tell you."

I laughed at the spunk of this ancestor I'd grown to love. I thought about his request and began to imagine a man who loved his family. As I pieced it together, I realized how William must have felt. He didn't want any of his descendents left off the tree.

I returned to my research and went through it with a fine-toothed comb. Some had died without marriages or children, and some grandchildren had not been able to continue the line. The descendents were not that prolific. Nonetheless, I did find a few names that hadn't been included on the tree.

Finally, satisfied I had fulfilled my responsibility, I reported back to William. "I have done everything I can to find all the family. I've taken their names to the temple and provided the necessary ordinances." Everything was in place. I waited.

While at my computer one day, still searching for William's parents, I tried a new website of burials. I paid a modest fee and found an entry—the right place and the right name. *William Gaze.* Wow! With some confusion as to why it hadn't been listed elsewhere, I phoned the local registration office to speak to the staff to ask why he hadn't appeared on the general index. The worker found the entry—the first name in a small book not included in the main national index.

I waited in great anticipation for the certificate, which would give more information. When it arrived, I found it to be an interesting death record. It was not his wife who registered his death, but the housekeeper where he was a butler. I then found his wife on the 1841 census.

As I trawled down the list of servants, there he was. *W. G.* Isn't it frustrating that family members can escape detection because they are registered with only initials?

The great news was that the death certificate included an age. I now knew when William was born—a piece of information that changed my whole research approach, as he was born much earlier than I had estimated.

With a definite date, it didn't take long for me to find his name slightly to the north and in the neighboring county of Gloucestershire. I had found him—and I knew who his parents were. *Gaze* is a Norfolk name and there are very few with that name outside that county, so I was in no doubt about the accuracy of my find.

What amused me most was that I decided to retire to Gloucestershire a year earlier with no idea that it was family territory. I didn't know why my heart leapt when I drove through the countryside and found myself literally singing at the sight of the hills and views. It seemed a little sentimental, but now I understood. Part of my bloodline had been here before.

Annie Made Me Cry

Alison M. Young-Herron, Dance Teacher—Washington, USA

My mother's father was Nels Johan Nelson, son of Johan Emanuel Nelson. Johan Emanuel was a big mystery to our family. We knew he was from Sweden and that he died in North Dakota when his son Nels was ten, but that was it.

Annie Fosmark

In 2001, I got serious about working on my mother's genealogy. One of the names I found was Nels Nelson's mother, Annie Fosmark, my great-grandmother—wife of the mysterious Johan. I knew nothing about her. She was only a small and hardly discernable face in a couple of very old family group photos my mother left me. I had the names of a few of Annie's ancestors, but for some reason, they had never attracted my attention.

While being baptized in the temple work on behalf of Annie (Anna Johannesdatter Fosmark Nelson, born 1866, Osteroy, Norway; died 1960, Toole, Montana), for no obvious reason, I began to cry. Up to that point, I'd experienced peaceful, happy feelings. The people with me at the temple felt something too—we all got emotional. The moment we were finished with Annie's work, the crying stopped. It was like someone turned off a faucet, and I went right back to being happy and peaceful. I was puzzled. Why had Annie made me cry? The emotions that came with my tears seemed like a mixture of joy and something else. I wondered if I would ever know what happened and why.

I had time for one endowment session before going home and decided I should do it for Annie Fosmark, since she obviously chose to accept the work. It was then I discovered an error: none of the work I'd done earlier for Annie had been recorded. I felt that I'd solved the mystery of my tears: Annie must have been upset that her baptism and confirmation hadn't been checked off and dated. But there was more to come.

Months went by, and my schedule crowded out further research. Then in December, I learned of a family-history book project taking shape within my father's side. A female cousin of his and her daughters needed my life history, family group sheets and family photos, and remembrances about my father and his parents from both me and my children. As I contemplated what a great thing this book would be for us all, I found myself wishing someone would compile such a book for my mother's family. Quickly deciding I was the logical person to take on the task, I jumped right in.

I made contact with many of my mother's relatives for the first time, which never failed to be a sweet experience. Best of all was the result that came from Uncle John mentioning that some Fosmarks had once lived near me in Washington State. This information led me to a round of phone calls that helped us discover a second cousin (Jack M. Fosmark) of my mother's from Oregon—a serious genealogist who had spent the last twenty-five years devoting himself to Fosmark family research.

Jack emailed me a picture of Annie's parents. There, from the computer screen, were my great-great-grandparents staring back at me.

In addition to bursting into tears, I learned that my mother reversed the names of Annie's parents, and the temple work had been done for her mother (Kari) as a male, and her father (Johannes) as a female! No wonder Annie was upset. Important details needed fixing.

I received many more remarkable photos. Two were about 100 years old, taken in North Dakota. Both were of huge Nelson/Fosmark gatherings, with the young widow Annie and her five children. And there was my grandfather Nels as a teenager, second from the left! I cried most of that day.

There was another Annie surprise in store. As I began digging through Mom's old family records and photos, I found two copies of a Lutheran prayer book. One had the name Lars Fosmark on the inside cover. It was signed by Johannes Johannesson Blomdal (Fosmark)— likely the only signature of my great-great-grandfather in existence.

Jack said Lars was Annie's brother. I scanned the page containing Johannes' signature and sent it to Jack, telling him that since there were two copies, I felt I should give that book to Lars's descendents. So Jack forwarded the scanned page and sent it to Lars's grandson, Richard (Dick) Puck, of California.

Within hours, I received an e-mail from a good friend, Patty, who I'd served with on the board of directors for a dance company in Seattle, Patty's message read, "Alison! Dick Puck is my father!" I think I sucked all the air out of the room at that moment. Woohoo! Patty (Patricia Puck Iverson) was my cousin!

The connections and blessings continued. I became acquainted with Patty's sister, Sara (Sara Puck Longworth). Sara visited the little farm/hamlet of Fossmark, Norway, where many distant cousins still reside. Then, in 2003, all the new-found cousins got together at a huge Fosmark reunion, with over one-hundred-and-fifty people in attendance, from all over the US, Canada, & Netherlands.

I'm so happy Annie made me cry that day in the temple.

Family Connections from eBay

Becky Jamison, Parish Administrator—Colorado, USA

One day I received an email from Ancestry.com's connection service sent by a young woman named Cristina. She explained she was searching eBay for items from Stafford, Kansas, USA, where she had relatives, when she came across a picture postcard for sale of a child identified as Thelma Lucille Steele, born April 1906, in Stafford, Kansas. After searching further in Ancestry.com, she found Thelma listed in my husband's family tree.

I wasn't familiar with anyone named Thelma L. Steele, but in examining the database, I discovered that Thelma was the sister-in-law to Anita Trump Cochran, aunt of my husband's first wife, Shelly Jaynes, for whom I've done family history research.

Shelly and I had spent eight hours the previous day going through nearly three hundred pictures given to her from the estate of her aunt Anita Cochran, so I called her about Cristina's message. I was amazed that this additional photo came into our lives at this particular time.

I replied to Cristina with thanks for sharing the eBay auction item with me and mentioned that I, too, was familiar with Stafford, Kansas, because my grandparents lived there and my mother graduated from Stafford High School in 1943.

Cristina wrote right back telling me her ancestors were in Stafford way before the years my mother was there. She said her great-grandmother Mary Josephine Smiley was born in 1888 and lived in Stafford.

Mary Josephine . . . *Smiley?*

The last name was *Smiley*? I had an Aunt Alberta Smiley (born September 1913) from Stafford, Kansas, who married my mother's oldest brother, Cleo Flanders (born July 1912, Barton, Kansas).

I hurriedly looked in my own database and found Cristina's Mary Josephine Smiley, who happens to be the first cousin of my aunt Berta's father, Frank Gerard Smiley.

I called Shelly again and told her there was more to this miraculous story. I also emailed Cristina with the news of our family connection, and immediately received her reply: "I can't believe it. I just can't believe it. I still can't believe it!"

Personally, I had no trouble believing it. This kind of thing happens to me frequently. When we have the help of our ancestors, all kinds of connections pop up in the most surprising places. Just think about it . . . in an act of genealogical kindness, a nice young woman wrote to advise me of an heirloom available on eBay that was connected to my husband's first wife's family. and then we discovered she was connected to *my* family.

Immediately prior to this discovery, I had written on my blog about all the cousins I'd found on Facebook who are the grandchildren of Aunt Berta Smiley and Uncle Cleo Flanders. I wrote about Anita Cochran and the abundance of heirlooms with which she has blessed Shelly Jaynes.

I think there are some very busy members of both my family and Shelly's family who have helped us in this genealogy research. How blessed we are.

A Whisper Away

Elizabeth Jane Roberts, Researcher and Educator—Gloucestershire, England

I swung my legs over the side of the bed and sat there, trying to make sense of the dream. I remember most of my dreams very clearly, but this one left me puzzled. Dreams are a common way for ancestors to leave messages, visit, or pass on information. In return, we like to help, but we do expect a fair share of clues. All I could grasp from the dream was the name Frances. *Frances who?* I kept thinking. *That's rather minimal information to work on. They must think I'm a genius.* Strangely, I knew Frances was female, as opposed to a male Francis.

My day allowed me to work on history research so I sat at my desk and pondered. I had done the praying, and now it was a matter of intelligent decision-making. How was I to find Frances without a surname to go by? I had been working on the Aldington, Kent, records so it seemed logical to go back to what I was already doing until I got a better idea. I opened the books and plodded on from where I left off the day before, looking at transcripts.

My Kent families are Drylands, Butchers, and Faggs—great names which I am passionately fond of. One village can connect in many ways. You add a wife then you find a brother-in-law; and then add his marriage and a wife's name, and then her parents, and it blossoms like a fruit tree. No day is long enough to satisfy the search. One village can connect with a web of relationships. As marriages made connections and christenings gave me parents' names, I moved back generation by generation.

Suddenly, a connection stood out. *Goodwin. Frances Goodwin.* Was this *the* Frances? She was connected to my tree, which made sense with the communication in my dream. I placed her on the tree and searched for her parents, their marriage, and finally her brothers and sisters.

By the end of the day, I had the entire family. I checked to see if Frances's family was on IGI and Family Search. Yes. As I went through her family names, all of their work seemed done, name after name. All were registered correctly—names, dates, places. I reviewed the finished sheet, tears trickling down my cheeks. Someone had called my name in my sleep and sought my ear. She had a special need, and I found it.

All her family names had been taken to the temple—all except *hers*.

That was why Francis sought permission to speak to me, here on earth, where I could do this unique work for her. Sometimes, we don't appreciate the reality of the power we hold to serve our ancestors until we are led by faith to do something so special. And sometimes we forget how close heaven is to earth—just a whisper away.

The Treasure Box and Little Elizabeth

Barbara Guerrant Walton—Vermont, USA

For well over a year, I searched without success for documentation of a marriage between my great-aunt Gussie Guerrant (born 1878, North Carolina; died 1950, South Rhodesia, Africa), and a man I believed to be her first husband, Charles Newton Lynch (born 1866, West Virginia; died 1904, Galveston, Texas).

Three years previously, I discovered a marker for Charles Newton Lynch in the Guerrant plot of the Green Hill Cemetery, in Danville, Virginia. I concluded that this Charles Newton Lynch was probably the first husband of Great-aunt Gussie, but had no proof except for his birth and death dates recorded on the gravestone. Family oral history said that Aunt Gussie married a Linch.

I'd learned from a distant relative in Australia about a rumor that the Lynch/Guerrant marriage produced a child named Elizabeth, who died very young. I searched genealogy sites for the birth or death of a young girl named Elizabeth Lynch in North Carolina, Virginia, and Louisiana where the couple were said to have lived. I could not find any records, but this little girl stayed in my heart.

A couple of weeks prior to my granddaughter's first youth trip to the Boston Temple, I sat pondering which family names to prepare for her to do proxy baptisms. As I contemplated these names, I received the strong impression I needed to research some cemetery records on the Internet. When I told my husband I was considering membership in one or more of the national websites that claim to have cemetery records, his reaction was, "Why join another site when the LDS Church has a great deal of information on cemeteries gleaned during the 1930s?" When I asked if the information was online, he said it was not. I considered requesting some films from the Family History Library, but still felt prompted to go to cemetery sites online.

A few days later, I ran into Linda Miller, our regional family history consultant. I asked if she could tell me how to find cemetery records online. She told me about a free website, www.findagrave.com, which might provide some useful information.

Upon returning home, I immediately went to my computer and pulled up the site. Much to my surprise, I came upon not only the name of a great-uncle, Daniel Guerrant, but also his picture and an elaborate obituary. Words simply cannot express my excitement and joy that Sunday afternoon. I wondered how someone could have a picture of my great-uncle and his obituary on a graveyard website. Did this mean an unknown distant relative was submitting information online?

At the bottom of the picture was a woman's name and contact information. I didn't recognize the name but decided to send an email. It turned out she wasn't a relative but an individual passionate about family history who dedicated much of her spare time to family-history. It soon became clear that she couldn't bear to see family-history records, old pictures, or scrapbooks left sitting around as junk or in antique shops.

In her adventures, this lovely lady came across a box of family-history information in an antique store in Rockingham County, North Carolina, and purchased it. The box contained priceless information about my great-grandfather, John Wyatt Guerrant, and numerous other relatives. There were records, certificates, a Bible, and scrapbooks filled with births, marriages, and obituaries clipped from newspapers over several decades. This lady took the box home, hoping one day to come across a relative for one or more of the families in the box.

We emailed back and forth, and I became increasingly excited as she described each treasure in the box—especially when she attached pictures. With some hesitation, I asked if she'd be willing to sell me the collection. She said she'd be happy to simply recover her costs, because she wanted the material to be in the hands of family.

Then began the longest ten-day wait of my genealogical research life while I waited for this priceless gift to arrive. When it finally came, I found that my benefactor had packed the box with great care and love for those long dead ancestors of mine. On top of the contents was a handwritten note that read, "I am so happy these treasures are finally going home to be with family. I guess I was meant to find them, so you could find me!"

In the treasure box, I found information going back some two hundred years, telling about relatives both known and unknown to me. But the discoveries that touched my heart most were two clippings in a newspaper documenting the marriage of Gussie and Charles, and birth and death dates of Mary Elizabeth Lynch (born April 1902, Danville, Virginia; died July 14, 1903, Jackson, Louisiana). There was also an obituary for Mary Elizabeth Lynch, and although it didn't mention her parents, I was able to connect the dots with the additional information it contained and determined that this was indeed the rumored daughter of Gussie and Charles Lynch who died at age two, at Jackson, Louisiana, on July 14, 1903.

I believe this treasure box was a priceless gift from the other side of the veil, and am grateful for the Spirit of Elijah and daily inspiration from the Holy Ghost that made this amazing discovery possible.

Astounding Meeting

Robert Richardson, Sydney Temple Coordinator—Australia

In 2008, while visiting family history sites in England, my wife and I went to Wigston, Leicestershire, where my great-great-grandmother Mary Hampson Walker lived. I wanted to go in the morning, but my wife had things to do, and we finally arrived in Wigston after three P.M.

I guessed Mary was christened at St. Wistan's Church in Moat Street in June 1819. All the gravestones stood along a narrow pathway around the church. A couple of stones carried the name *Langham*, my great-grandmother's mother's maiden name, but there was little else of interest.

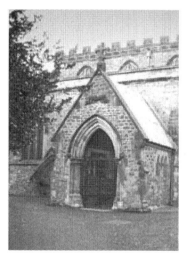

We noticed two men inside the church. When they broke up, one continued to look at church artifacts and the other came over to us. He was the church warden, so we asked if we could examine the records. That wasn't possible, so we took some photos and walked outside.

Then the other man came out, and as he passed us, he asked if we were doing family history. We answered, "Yes."

He then asked, "What families?"

I replied, "Walker."

He said, "Any others?"

"Langham."

He looked at us, astounded, then stated his name was Jonathon Langham and that he was also researching the Langham family. On realizing we were related, we shared information not previously available to either of us.

The meeting was more than a remarkable coincidence in view of the fact that I'd originally intended to visit the church in the morning and it was late in the afternoon before our paths crossed. In our later exchange of emails, Jonathon referred to our meeting as being "Quite spooky." Later, on meeting again outside the Langham family church in Kilby, Leicestershire, Jonathon indicated he lived only five miles or so from Wigston all his life, and that was the first time he ever went inside that church.

That day, two arms of the same family came together for the first time in almost two hundred years. Is there any doubt the spirit of Elijah is well and truly alive?

A Dream Come True

Ewan Harbrecht Mitton, Former Opera and Concert Artist—Utah, USA

Scribes in Germany recorded my ancestral line. While researching one day, I came upon a microfilm with writing that was difficult to read. When I took it to the experts at the library desk, they couldn't read it either. Since it covered very important data for my research, I prayed about it that night. As dawn came, when I was still half-asleep, I had a dream.

I was standing in the doorway of a church—somehow I knew I was in Germany—and a white horse drove up, drawing a white, shiny sleigh trimmed with polished brass. A beautiful young woman sat on a white seat with fur around it. A white fur robe lay across her lap. She was holding the reins and smiled at me as she stopped the fine-looking horse by the door where I stood.

The lady was more beautiful than any movie star. Her skin was white and transparent. Her eyes sparkled ebony black, with long black eyelashes. Her lips were red, probably from the cold wind.

She said, "Hello Ewan," so I asked for her name.

"You will know when you find me on the microfilm," she replied.

"Oh, then you are a relative of mine?"

"Yes," she replied, "You have missed me because of your 'Scribbly Scribe,' as you call him. You must understand. He was our pastor. He was very old, and trying to record and write in a cold little room up in the tower. He did the best he could."

She continued, "Let me help you. Here, this is how Harbrecht looks, and Stark, and Bloed."

She showed me a page with how these names looked in his handwriting, then added, "Now look carefully and practice reading this script, and you will find *lots* of us children there."

I thanked her and told her this information would certainly help.

Her long, wavy black hair cascaded over her shoulders and down her back, flowing in the wind as she drove off. I never before saw such an elegant woman.

I awakened, went right to my record book, and wrote down the names exactly as she had showed me.

I went to the family history library, got that microfilm, and discovered the priest had made duplicate copies of each entry. They were all in the same handwriting covering over twenty years of history. But in some places, where I'd been unable to read a name, such as *Bloed,* because of a big ink blotch, in the duplicate copy, I could read it plainly.

I took this page to the desk and asked if these names could be right. They confirmed that they were, even though the writing was hard to make out at first. So I sat down at the microfilm and continued reading.

There, on the first entry, was the very page the lady in my dream had shown me. I thought she had simply shown me an example of this man's writing, but I got the Harbrecht chills (what my genealogist friend and I felt whenever we came across my family names) as I received a confirmation that I was looking at *her* name on the page: Marie Helena Stark, the beautiful young lady in the white sleigh.

Marie Helena's mother was Hedwig Harbrecht, my great-great-great-grandfather Leonard Harbrecht's sister. I knew then why it was necessary for me to find this microfilm. The priest's records covered over twenty-five years of valuable information. I now had all the family correctly recorded.

Some years later, I was able to visit that very town in Germany and go in that same church. I stood in the doorway and looked out on the scene from my dream. It was springtime, not winter, but it was just as thrilling to see.

I went through the temple on behalf of my angel, Marie Helena. On coming out of the water after the baptism, I saw a young girl crying.

I asked why and she said, "I saw the lady for whom you did the baptism. She looked like Elizabeth Taylor the movie star, with long black hair, white skin, and red lips. Oh, so beautiful."

I said, "Yes, I know your description of her, and it's just the way I saw her in a dream. Always remember to hold this sacred and let it strengthen your testimony. Never deny what you have seen. This *is* the work of the Lord." We hugged.

I am the only child in my family, and the only member of The Church of Jesus Christ of Latter-day Saints on my mother's side. I always felt I had this mission to find my ancestors. I have now researched over five thousand names. What a joy it is to feel the Spirit of Elijah and to do this great work.

The Census Dream

Amie Borst, Writer—Washington DC, USA

A few years ago, I was doing some family history research with my parents and sister. My mother had been searching for her great-grandfather for a long time, and she knew very little about his son, her grandfather. My mom encouraged me to start looking for her great-grandfather, but I procrastinated. Although I had done temple work, I'd never stepped foot into a family-history library.

One night, while Mom was visiting my home in Virginia, I had a dream in which I clearly saw a document. It had a list of names, which I guessed was a family. The parents were offset to the left a bit, and the names below were their children. I saw my grandfather's name (Mom's father). It said, "Arthur." Above it was another name, Clifford, who I assumed was the father. To the right were dates and occupations. I had no idea what all this meant, but remember struggling the whole night to memorize the paper and the names on it.

Next morning, I told my mom about the dream and said I had the strong feeling we should go to the stake family-history center in Centerville. Previously, Mom searched in her small ward family history center in New York, where she was the librarian, and had never found anything on this family. When we reached the research center, I told the workers there about my dream, and began searching documents.

Finally, they pulled up a census. When I saw the document, my heart started racing—the image from my dream flashed in my mind. I had never seen a census before in my life. Yet this document was the one from my dream. Without a doubt. Everything about it was the same. Even the handwriting.

I scrolled down until I saw the name from my dream: my great-grandfather, Clifford Cummins, and below it, his son (my grandfather, my mom's father), Arthur Cummins. I started crying. And so did Mom. This was the first document she had seen in all her years of searching that contained pertinent information about her family. It was our first step in finding her great-grandfather.

As we searched more documents that day, we finally found Mom's great-grandfather's name and family on a census. Because of my dream, we were able to find the first census containing my grandfather's name, and then trace back from one census to another, since we now had birth dates and cities to help.

I believe the Spirit led me to something I would recognize. If I'd just seen my great-great-grandfathers name, it would have meant nothing to me, and I probably would have ignored it. But because I saw that document with my grandfather's name, Arthur, I recognized it and knew someone was trying to reach me.

Discovering John Peyton Overton

James W. Petty, AG, CG, B.A., B.S., Professional Genealogist—Utah, USA

I was working with Harry McCoy, a convert to the LDS Church in Salt Lake City whose family came from West Virginia. He had a great-grandfather, John Peyton Overton, of Parkersburg, West Virginia, who had been a Union veteran of the Civil War.

After many efforts searching the Overton line, we were unable to find the origins of this ancestor or any evidence of him prior to 1863. Then one evening, as I researched John P. Overton at the Family History Library, I considered the possibility that he may have started the war as a Confederate soldier, as did many of the men serving from West Virginia, and then joined the Union when West Virginia seceded from Virginia in 1863. Suddenly, the pieces began falling into place. I learned that John originally enlisted in the 16th Virginia Regiment as a Confederate soldier from Amherst County, Virginia.

I was excited about this discovery, and that evening, as I drove home, a feeling of peace swept over me. A voice in my mind said, "Thank you. Please tell my grandson I wish to receive my work." I was overwhelmed and immediately redirected my travel to visit the McCoy home. I arrived there late, asked to see Brother McCoy and for all the family to be present. I then related my experience of the day, and the promptings I felt within that last hour. Tears expressed the feeling of everyone present. Research was completed and temple ordinances performed. But the story doesn't stop there.

A year later, Harry McCoy contacted me and related the rest of the story. He was an attorney by profession and served as a member of the high council in his stake. On one occasion, he was speaking to members of his own ward. He resolved to speak on genealogy and temple work and to tell the story of his great-grandfather John Peyton Overton:

> I stood and began speaking, and almost immediately saw my wife and daughter in the audience. They were weeping. I didn't know what the problem was, so I continued and eventually completed my talk.
>
> After the meeting closed, I went to them concerned about their distress. They explained together that when I rose to speak another man stood next to me. He remained by me throughout my talk, and was gone when I sat down. Although they never saw him before, they both knew he was my great-grandfather John Peyton Overton.

The Right Cemetery

Shirley Rothas—Florida, USA

Michael Messner and his wife, Salome Reister, were married about 1720. They and two of their sons, Christian (1724–1807) and Casper (1722–1781) emigrated from Brotzingen, Baden-Durlach, to America, arriving at Philadelphia on the ship *Friendship* on 20 September 1738. They settled in Lancaster County, Pennsylvania, USA.

My father's family had an interest in family history for many years, so I knew all about these parents and two sons who came from Germany and settled in Pennsylvania, including the fact that their temple work had been done.

However, a few years ago, I woke up with the thought, *Clean out the cedar chest.* I tried to go back to sleep, but the thought wouldn't go away. In the morning, I looked through the cedar chest. There I found information on four children who had died before the family immigrated, and a son who married and chose to stay in Germany. An elderly family member shared this information at a family reunion, but it had been neglected for twenty years.

On my husband's side, my mother-in-law did not know a lot about her family. Her mother (Sarah Mae Whitman, born 1898, West Chester, Pennsylvania) died when she was ten. Her grandmother, Gertrude E. Whitman (born 1878, West Chester) died the next year. Shortly before she died in 1989, my mother-in-law told me where she thought her mother was buried. My mother and I searched a cemetery with the name given to us, but it was not the right one. Because I do not live in that state, I didn't think much about it over the years.

Then, two years ago, we were going home for a class reunion. A few nights before our trip, I awoke with the persistent thought to look in the bottom drawer of my bedroom dresser. In there, I found a small piece of paper with the name of a cemetery. I don't even remember writing the name down.

On our trip, no one was able to tell us where the cemetery was, but my husband and I decided to drive around and see what we could find. By the time we discovered the right cemetery, it was raining, and we really didn't want to walk through the rain without an umbrella, so we drove through the cemetery.

Just as we were about to give up the search, there were the headstones we were looking for, right at the edge of the lane. We not only found the grave of my husband's grandmother and great-grandmother, but also a great-aunt and uncle.

I believe our relatives know of our interest in them, and they know where we can find the information we need to have saving ordinances done on their behalf. If we listen, they will help us. I just wish it wasn't in the middle of the night when they feel I will listen.

On a Cold and Misty Mountain

John Counsel, Business Consultant/Trainer/Author—Australia

Despite valiant efforts over many years, especially by our father and by my sister Marg, who made several lengthy trips to the United Kingdom and Europe in search of our ancestors, the progress made was mainly within a very limited number of lines, mostly on my mother's side and, to a lesser extent, on my father's maternal side. Then, in January 1979, one significant event seemed to be the key that unlocked the treasure trove.

After serving a senior couple mission with Mum in the New Zealand Temple in 1977, Dad returned home in deteriorating health. In early 1978, he was diagnosed with brain tumors, lung cancer, and melanomas throughout his body. Any of these cancers could have ended his life. As weeks turned into months, it became clear to us as a family that the Lord had work waiting for him on the other side of the veil.

During this time, I sold my business in our home town of Wonthaggi, took a position with a company in Melbourne, and lived in that city during the week. This was prior to Dad's illness, which later required his transfer to the Repatriation Hospital for war veterans in Heidelberg, a Melbourne suburb. By coincidence—or not—my apartment was located in Balwyn, and my new job in East Brunswick. I passed the hospital twice a day on my way to and from the office, and most days, I called in to spend time with Dad on my way home from work.

More often than not, Dad was asleep, but it was calming to simply sit by his bed and observe him, reflecting on our life together and his legacy to me as a son.

There were occasions when I sensed someone else close to Dad's bed, but I never saw anyone. I learned from Marg that shortly before his death, Dad began introducing her to visitors and staff as his "elder" daughter—something he'd never done before. Our baby sister, Robyn, had died from Rh-factor complications shortly after birth, when I was three or four years old. This explained the unseen presence near Dad's bed and the serenity and calm that set him apart in the hospital ward. At a time when he should have been in excruciating pain, like so many of the veterans in the terminal cancer ward, his suffering was practically non-existent. Several doctors and psychologists wanted to understand Dad's extraordinary resilience and our own ability to cope with his condition without despair or even despondency, so they interviewed us separately.

Prior to Dad's death, our mother spoke with him about how important it was for him to help us from the other side so we could begin to make serious progress tracing all the lines of our family history.

Try as we might, some lines—notably the Counsel line itself—seemed to elude us. Often we felt like we were taking three steps forward and two steps back in every direction we attempted. We knew the Counsel family had come to Australia from Ireland in the early 19th century, but we couldn't find from where in Ireland or to where in Australia. There were dead-ends everywhere.

Our brother Peter lived and worked at the Monash University campus in Churchill, in the Latrobe Valley of Victoria, about two hundred kilometers east of Melbourne. One day in the early 1980s, Mum went to stay with Peter for a few days and was introduced to a post-graduate student friend of Peter's, who turned out to be Paul Counsel from Tasmania. He informed Mum that the north-west of Tasmania was full of Counsels, that there was a Mount Counsel in the Franklin-Gordon Wilderness region and another on King Island, in Bass Strait, named by the first surveyor-general of Tasmania. Prior to 1856, this area was known as Van Diemen's Land, when the surveyor-general first toured the island state.

This was good news, but it wasn't until 1985 that I found myself in Hobart, the state capital, on business. It was the first of many trips in the next couple of years, when I would stay for three days with my long-time friends, Keith and Dawn Sayers and their family.

I recall arriving at Hobart airport on my second trip, wondering how I could go about contacting someone in the Counsel family. When I made my way to the pick-up point for my rental car, my eyes were drawn to an unusually large, diamond-shaped rental-car sticker on the rear passenger-side window. The director-general of transport had signed it—and he was a Counsel. That was a promising start.

On my next trip south, I took my mother with me. I had learned that the national shipping archives in Hobart held the records of immigrants and convicts to Van Diemen's Land since the late 1700s, and Mum decided to come with me to spend time exploring the records. She had no luck, and we returned home, despondent.

On my final trip to Hobart, my six-year-old daughter Naomi accompanied me. It was the middle of winter, so the flight was rough. We arrived mid-afternoon and settled into our home-away-from-home at Midway Point, to the north of Hobart.

I stared through the front window of the house in the direction of Hobart, and could see through the intervening hills to Mount Wellington, the snow-capped peak that stood immediately against the south-western fringe of Hobart. At that moment, I had the overwhelming impression I needed to meet someone on that mountain during my visit. I had no idea who, where, or why, but couldn't get rid of the feeling.

On previous trips to Hobart with my young girls, I scheduled the last day of each visit for a sightseeing trip to the summit of Mount Wellington, then back to Hobart for lunch. This was always followed by a scenic drive to Port Arthur, the ruins of the original convict penal settlement, before heading home next morning to Melbourne, one hour north across Bass Strait.

Early on the final day, I looked out once again at Mount Wellington, and my heart fell. It was a cold, wet day, and thick mist shrouded the entire mountain. I wondered about the wisdom of driving up there in such conditions, but felt impelled to go. Naomi was quite happy to accompany me on the dreary journey.

We stopped at every ranger hut, every car park, toilet block, lookout, or other facility on our ascent. We appeared to be the only two people on the entire mountain. When we reached the summit car park, sleet was falling, and the clouds made it dangerous to venture too far from the car. We quickly scouted around the summit, and after finding no trace of life, wound our way back down again, stopping at every point once more to double-check for human presence.

Nothing. There was no one anywhere.

Discouraged, we decided to head back to Hobart, grab some lunch, and then drive to Port Arthur, with the promise of a ride on the Bush Mill miniature railway. As we were about to turn northward, a sudden, savage gust of wind flattened the tall shrubbery on the opposite side of the T-intersection, revealing a very old, dilapidated sign pointing south, reading, "Shops 1 mile." That sounded like a good alternative, since Naomi was hungry and wanted to buy souvenirs. It would also save us a trip back into the city.

But when we reached the one-mile mark (1.6 km), we found that a large hotel-motel complex had replaced the shops adjacent to Settler's Green Tourist Village. The old sign was obviously outdated by decades. Still, we could shop for souvenirs, so we stopped and entered the building. Once again, nobody was there.

We waited for awhile, and then I moved to the barn door that led into the tourist park proper. I noticed an older man at the opposite end of the green, further down the sloping hillside. We decided to choose some souvenirs, leave a note with the correct amount of money, and leave.

We were finalizing our purchases when the elderly chap entered the store, apologized profusely for not attending to us, and took our money. After chatting amiably for a few minutes, Naomi reminded me that we still hadn't eaten. As we moved to the door, I turned to our host, held out my hand, and for some unknown reason, said, "By the way, my name is John Counsel."

The words exited my mouth unbidden. I did not intend to mention my name, but there it was. It was the strangest experience. And it had a startling impact on our new friend. His mouth fell open for several seconds before he said, "Well, isn't that interesting? My name is Viv Rogers. I'm the family historian for the Rogers clan in Tasmania—and one of our four principal lines is the Counsels."

In the next few minutes I'd secured his name and contact information, with a promise to put my sister Marg in touch with him the moment I returned home.

So there was my answer—the person I was supposed to meet on the mountain. Over the next few years, that connection proved incredibly fruitful for us, unleashing a torrent of names, locations, dates, and relationships dating back to the first known user of the Counsel surname, William Counsel, personal advisor to William the Conqueror.

Six Years Missing

John Counsel, Business Consultant/Trainer/Author—Australia

Despite rapid progress with the Counsel family line after our father died, a troubling inconsistency appeared for which we could find no explanation. We learned that one ancestor from County Louth in Ireland left his homeland, travelled to Australia, and found success. He then sent back to Ireland for his five brothers and their families, who also emigrated to Australia in the early nineteenth century, all settling in Tasmania, at least initially.

The quandary? At a time when a voyage to Australia took around six months, this original Counsel had arrived six *years* after he left Ireland. We could find no explanation for this massive discrepancy, and were beginning to wonder whether, in fact, this person was actually two different people. It was puzzling and frustrating, and we could find no clarification or direction.

In January 2007, my family relocated to Melbourne. Not long after our arrival, I saw a notice for a free evening seminar on Tasmanian Family History Records by an expert in the field. I hoped the teacher would explain some peculiarities that caused confusion when tracing genealogy in Tasmania. I decided to attend in the hope of finding a resolution to my own puzzle.

I was disappointed when none of the material presented provided any clues, but I decided to ask the presenter if she had any suggestions that could help me. She advised me to study the report written by the first surveyor-general of Van Diemen's Land and see if he mentioned anything helpful. As an afterthought, she pointed to a very old book on a nearby table, saying it was a copy of that very report. I felt impressed to browse the book for as long as I could before the meeting closed.

The first surveyor-general's report is a journal-style record of his journey around Van Diemen's Land in the early 1800s. I began reading from the start. From the first couple of paragraphs I learned the following:

- He left Hobart Town late in the afternoon and crossed the Derwent River.
- He travelled a short distance to Sorell, where he stayed the night with Mr. Andrew Counsel and his business partner, recently arrived in the colony from the Cape of Good Hope colony (South Africa), *where they had been farmers for the past 6 years!*

There was our answer, in the first paragraphs of the book—a simple explanation of why that bothersome six-year gap existed.

After spending six year in an African colony, Andrew Counsel arrived in Australia and sent for his five brothers still living in Ireland, and all of them joined him in Van Diemen's Land. Sometime later, two of the brothers left Tasmania and traveled to the mainland, where two distinct branches of the family exist to this day. One line uses the spelling *Counsel*, while the other uses *Counsell*.

These incidents could be attributed to sheer coincidence. Personally, I find it impossible to dismiss such consistencies as anything less than inspired. They are too many, too often, too consistent, and too remarkable to be mere serendipity.

One Kind Act

Luckie Daniels, Interactive Project Manager—Georgia, USA

Over the years, I have been the beneficiary of small and large genealogical random acts of kindness, many of which have led me to believe my ancestors are masters at executing their well-laid plans.

Out of all the gifts I have received, none stands out like the family bible that once belonged to my paternal great-great-grandmother Myrtle Perry Cobb, and Grandmother Lovella Cobb Daniels, which a complete stranger named Debbie returned to me.

Even more amazing to me was the time span. There were five years between the day Debbie posted a note about the Bible on the Roots Web message board, and the day I Google-searched for the surnames *Daniels* and *Cobb*—five is enough years for her note to have been erased or lost in cyberspace.

The people listed as appearing in this Cobb family Bible were my grandfather and grandmother, father and his siblings, all of whom I had never met. There were also aunts and uncles I never knew existed. It held four generations of my paternal grandmothers.

I had given up hope of ever knowing anything about this side of my family. Through the Creator's grace, and one act of kindness, I am now healing a void that I believed could never heal.

Discovering the Impossible

Jo Archer Arnspiger, Genealogist and Website Designer—Arizona, USA

My husband Gene and I visited Nicholasville, Jessamine County, Kentucky, in 2000 to attend the 1st Annual History Fest. It was our first time in Kentucky, even though I had researched Gene's family for twenty-five years. The Ernspiger/Arnspiger family moved to this area in 1792. Jessamine County is a beautiful, rural region of the Blue Grass country of Kentucky. The Arnspigers settled in the German area known as Chattersville on the east and west forks of Jessamine creek.

The family lived in this area for about seventy-five years. Local historian and cemetery expert Howard Teater published three books of cemetery surveys containing over forty thousand names. But there was not *one* Arnspiger name in any of those books.

One of Howard Teater's surveys was for an old, neglected cemetery located on the Otis Wilder Farm on Short Shun Pike, southwest of Nicholasville, the Grow Cemetery. He found four stones there—none of them Arnspigers.

My question was always, "Where are they?"

During our visit, we went on a scheduled tour of what was fondly named Abraham Houser's Mill. This was the original mill structure built in 1800 or so by pioneer Abraham Houser Senior. Land owned by the Arnspiger family in the early 1800s was just down the creek from the Houser Mill.

While on the tour, Gene struck up a conversation with Bill Kinkle, owner of the land, and asked if he was aware of any other cemeteries in the area. He replied that he remembered one "from years before" just down and across the creek and would be happy to guide us. We quickly agreed, even though it meant leaving the tour group. Bill led us out to the road, around the bend, and over the creek, turning into nothing more than a path past a large, old, dilapidated house and up to a barn. From there we went in Bill's truck through a hayfield to a stand of trees. There was the old cemetery, completely overgrown with trees, high grass and numerous vines.

We started looking around and found several fieldstones, but most were unreadable. There were two large, well-preserved stones for Grow girls and a small double stone for twins who were also from the Grow family, just as Howard's books mentioned. While digging through the grass and vines, Gene found a marker with a different type of stone—whiter not granite, like the others—and with some legible letters, the most prominent being a *P*, and then what he thought was a *U*. He called me over, and we tried to make out more, but lichen and weathering made it difficult. I took a couple of pictures but didn't really think this was what we were looking for. We explored a little longer then decided we should find the tour.

We went up to the Moravian cemetery, which was next on the tour, but we'd already missed the group. We proceeded to the next stop on the tour: Wilmore Christian Church, a picturesque white building situated in a beautiful location. Still no sign of our tour group. A woman working in the churchyard said she hadn't seen anyone and wasn't aware of a planned visit, but the group arrived as we were about to leave. The woman was more than happy to open the church for the tour group.

Gene decided to remain outside, talking with some of the other members of the group and having no real interest in the church. As I entered, I imagined our ancestors from a hundred and fifty years ago filling this small building on a bright Sunday morning with buggies outside and men, woman and children attending services. Then I

noticed the beautiful portrait of Jesus
Christ behind the altar. It was the same
picture that hung in Gene's mother's
bedroom at home.

A few minutes later, Gene entered the
church and immediately noticed the
picture. He sat down and related the
following story to me. His father, Eugene,
who was a Lutheran, had his own ideas of
worshipping God. In 1956 in Chicago,
Eugene had some plasterwork done on a
house the family had purchased. He became involved in a debate with
the plasterer regarding religion and worship.

Finally the plasterer said, "Okay, if you're right, then ask God to tell
you." Eugene agreed and that night asked God to let him know. The
following morning, the doorbell rang. The real estate agent who sold
Eugene the house over a month ago stood outside. She had brought a
housewarming gift—a painting of Jesus. To Eugene, it was his answer
from God, and he believed it for the rest of his life. This picture of
Jesus hung in their home until Eugene's death and was the exact
replica of the one hanging in the church in Wilmore, Kentucky, in the
church of his ancestors.

We entered this church and saw the picture less than an hour after
leaving the old cemetery and the unidentified headstone. Were Gene's
father and grandfather trying to tell him something? It seemed oddly
coincidental.

Saturday night and all day Sunday, we talked about the cemetery and
the unidentified tombstone. Gene couldn't get it out of his mind, so we
decided to contact Howard again about going back to the cemetery,
this time with the proper equipment for cemetery exploration: trowel,

baby powder, shaving cream, and gentle brushes for highlighting obscure writing on the stones. Howard agreed to go on Tuesday morning.

Monday was a restless day for Gene. He was convinced that the letters we'd seen on the tombstone were P and U.

Was it possible that two west-coast city slickers could waltz into Jessamine County and find the gravestone of their pioneer ancestor who died one-hundred-and-seventy-eight years ago? It seemed possible to us. After all, no one recorded any of this family before. Why couldn't we be the ones—two people who really cared?

Monday night, it began to rain; not just a little rain, lots of rain, thunder and lightning. It rained through the night and was still raining in the morning. I was concerned about how much exploring we could do, but we drove on over to Howard's house anyway at our arranged time. Bill Kinkle from Houser Mill wanted to come along again to see what else we could find, so we picked him up on our way. Sometime during this drive, Gene noticed that his watch had stopped.

When we arrived at the farm, the driving became challenging, the path muddy and slick. As we were ready to head up the hay pasture path, the last stretch before the cemetery, the rain stopped. I thought, *Thank you, now we could explore the cemetery without getting soaked.* We switched vehicles, using Bill's truck for better traction, and proceeded up the mud path.

On reaching the old cemetery, Gene took us directly to the stone. Howard started his magic with shaving cream and a trowel—spreading on the cream, then gently toweling off the excess. Then Gene sprinkled baby powder over the same area and lightly brushed it until the inscription stood out. The letters were P and E.

Then Howard said, "Okay, there's a date. Looks like twenty-two."

I jumped and squeaked, "Twenty-two! Paul died in 1822." As we worked with the stone, the text became clearer: *P.E. died July 18, 1822.* We had found the headstone of Gene's 4th great-grandfather, Paul Ernspiger, or Arnspiger, as we now spell it.

I experienced awe, excitement, amazement, and fulfillment of a twenty-five year dream—absolute elation. What were the chances? This was a once-in-a-lifetime moment.

We continued looking through the cemetery for a long time. I took numerous pictures, and then we headed for Howard's car. And guess what? Down came the rain. Hard. Gene also noticed his watch was now working, but it was two hours behind—about how long we spent at the cemetery. Coincidence?

The unbelievable number of events and coincidences that occurred in helping us find this stone were incomprehensible.

We concluded that seven men—Eugene Steeves (Gene's father), Eugene Nettles, George William, Gabriel, Michael and Paul Arnspiger—all led us to that site and that stone.

To stand on the same ground on which this family stood, to pay homage to a true pioneer—Paul Ernspiger, Revolutionary War soldier, husband and father—will always be the highlight of my genealogical journey.

As Gene and I stood over the grave, I thought about Michael Arnspiger with his wife and children, Mary Bruner Arnspiger, wife of Paul Arnspiger, and Paul's other children, all standing on this same ground years ago. Now they are all looking down at us saying, "Finally, thank you."

We planned on leaving Jessamine County the next day and doing some other sightseeing, but we couldn't go. We felt drawn to revisit the cemetery and got permission to return the next day.

After five or six hours of further searching, we found another gravestone, almost completely buried in weeds and dirt, leaning precariously into a three-foot groundhog hole. It was right next to the *P.E.* stone, and the inscription read *J. Arnspiger* (Paul's grandson, one of Michael Arnspiger's four sons who died young). I was extremely excited.

To me, as the genealogist who needs as much proof as possible, this was the icing on the cake. Initials on a gravestone are not conclusive. Even though in my gut I knew the stone was Paul's, on a logical level, there was still room for doubt. But with a second marker in the same row, right next to *P.E.* with the Arnspiger surname? I was sure, absolutely sure, we had found Paul Ernspiger.

There are no words to convey the emotional experience of standing in that wild, overgrown cemetery looking at the headstone of Paul, a man for whom I'd been searching for twenty-five years. A man I have grown to know, love and respect as my own ancestor.

There is no logical explanation for our success in finding the stone. Gene and I truly believe we were the recipients of paranormal energy—his ancestors grabbing us by the ear, figuratively speaking, and leading us to the spot.

Getting to Know Vira Ann

G. G. Vandagriff, Author—Utah, USA

My grandmother knew nothing about her father's family. I looked for her father on censuses for years. Finally, an odd detail that didn't fit led me to look for him in Colorado in 1880. I knew he was from Illinois, but someone somewhere said he was from Colorado. I eventually found that he had lived in Colorado with his grandparents, Vira Ann and Jonas Barber.

As I looked into their lives and pedigrees, I found Vira Ann and Jonas to be remarkable people who founded seven pioneer settlements, always building a mill and a church. When things got too civilized, they moved to an unsettled area and began again. They ended up in Colorado, where they founded Golden. I thought this woman must be special to have endured so much and raised a family at the same time. I really wanted to get to know her, especially since I'd traced her genealogy back to the Mayflower.

One night, I prayed a very different kind of prayer—to see her face and learn more about her life. I prayed to know her. I realize this sounds crazy, but I just felt so close to her.

The next day, an unknown cousin called me. Her name was Joyce, and she found me by a circular route involving many other people. She was Vira Ann's favorite granddaughter's favorite granddaughter. Joyce had pictures, a quilt made by Vira Ann, and tons of stories. Best of all, she lived only one hundred miles away.

My prayer had been answered virtually immediately.

We met at a halfway point the next day, and I saw Vira Ann's face for the first time. Joyce even gave me a quilt square Vira Ann had stitched, and Joyce shared so many stories that I couldn't write them down fast enough.

The most amazing story was that Vira Ann made nine trips across the plains without her husband, at the head of huge wagon trains containing her belongings. I think she preferred the bright lights of Rock Island, Illinois, where they had a farm to the mountains of Colorado.

Led by a Confederate Flag

Ron Hendry—Utah, USA

While attending a funeral with my father and brother in Florida, I took the opportunity to visit the cemetery in Leesburg, where I'd heard Dad's great-grandfather on his grandmother's side was buried.

Dad was the oldest of seven children, and his father died at age forty when Dad was fourteen. Dad hadn't been to this graveyard before and knew little about his family history.

We hunted all over the old part of the cemetery but couldn't find a grave for Obed Fussell. At one point, not far from our car, we passed a grave marked with a flag sticking out.

"Look, that one's a Confederate," I commented to Dad. The headstone was unreadable, so we didn't stop, but kept on searching.

Eventually, having come full circle, my brother David shouted he'd found a grave for an infant Fussell.

As we hurried to look, I noticed that it wasn't far from the grave with a flag. I squinted more carefully at the name on the flagged tombstone, and made out the word *Obed*. Further inspection showed it was indeed that of my great-great-grandfather, Obed Fussell. Since this was the only flag in the whole graveyard, I'm convinced someone was helping us find him.

From that discovery, we were able to find Obed's wife, Louisa, and six children who died in infancy. As we recorded the names, I kept getting the feeling there was more, and that Dad's grandmother, Sarah Sussanah Fussell Hendry, was also in this cemetery. But we couldn't find her tombstone anywhere, so we left.

About twenty miles out from the graveyard, the thought came to check out www.findagrave.com on my cell phone. I did, and sure enough, Sarah's grave was listed as being at the cemetery we'd just left. We drove back and were able to find both Sarah and her husband, John A. Hendry.

I later discovered Obed's wife's father, Evander Lee, also in the same graveyard, and learned that he founded the town of Leesburg. This opened up a whole new line of ancestor's names to record and link into our family history.

My Father Gave Me My Identity Back

Sandra Taliaferro, Paralegal Specialist—Georgia, USA

I never knew my father.

Those words haunted me all through my childhood and most of my adult life.

As an African-American, the possibility of tracing my paternal ancestry was never an avenue I thought I could pursue with any success. A cursory search on Ancestry.com under the surname "Tolbert" did not yield any results that fit the few facts I learned over the years. I assumed I would not be able to find anything, although I longed to know my roots.

One day, while looking through some old photos and papers, I discovered two telegrams dated the day I was born. Both contained the surname "Taliaferro." The name triggered something. I had a vague memory of my mother telling me about my birth, about the hospital spelling my father's last name incorrectly on my birth certificate. I remembered knowing from an early age that my father's correct

surname was *Taliaferro*, not *Tolbert* as stated on the certificate, and he pronounced it "Toliver." I assumed the pronunciation accounted for the hospital's mistake. From conversations with my mother, I learned the names of my father's mother and his siblings.

Armed with these facts—and renewed determination—I rejoined Ancestry.com and

John Lawrence Taliaferro

began another search.

This time, on the 1930 census, I was able to locate my father (John Lawrence Taliaferro, born February 1, 1921, Cartersville, Georgia, USA) with his parents, brother, and sister. All the names fit with my information. What a thrill!

Searching back, I was able to locate my grandfather (John Robert Taliaferro, born 1875, Fulton, Georgia, USA) and his parents in the 1920, 1910, 1900 and 1880 census records.

John Robert Taliaferro

I also found my great-grandparents in the 1870 census. A few households away was another Taliaferro (Toliver) family. Could these be my great-great-grandparents? I felt confident all the relatives I had found so far were my ancestors, but there was no way to connect this last family from the 1870 census to my ancestors.

I turned to the Taliaferro message board on Ancestry.com in hopes of finding someone researching my Taliaferros. I went through each message one by one and then . . . BINGO! Someone was looking for any relatives of my father's parents.

I could not believe my tired eyes. It turns out this message was posted by my father's brother's daughter—my cousin—in June of 1999. She was no longer a member of Ancestry.com, so it was amazing I found her, right here in the same city and state where I live.

I did a search for her name, found several people with that name, and decided to send a letter to each one in the hopes of finding the author of the message. She turned out to be the very first person to whom I sent a letter.

After an initial email and phone conversation, she sent me an article written about our grandfather, which confirmed all the names I found in the census records. This article also confirmed that the male Taliaferro living in the household near my great-grandfather in the 1870 census was, in fact, my great-great-grandfather.

I have now been able to trace that great-great-grandfather and his son, my great-grandfather, to their slaveholder family in Georgia.

I finally discovered the family of the father I never knew. I could not have asked for more—but I did get more. After contacting that cousin from the message board, I had a new family from my paternal side: four first cousins, an aunt (my father's sister), and a *brother*.

My brother Bernard and I officially met July 2005. We have been inseparable since that day. On our first meeting, we had an instant connection.

In 2006, Bernard moved backed to Atlanta to live with me. He is my best friend and my protector. We are without a doubt soul mates. Because he grew up with our father, he is able to share memories of him with me.

Somehow, we both know that our father led me to my brother at just the right time in our lives.

In September 2005, I legally changed my surname to Taliaferro—a long, overdue correction of a life-altering mistake. I never felt complete but didn't know why. I always felt something was missing. That missing link was my family—my true identity.

An Accident and a Missing Link
Anita Harmon, Artist—Utah, USA

My grandparents on my father's side went on a big genealogy trip, visiting different places where our ancestors had lived. After a month of traveling and gathering copies of all kinds of important documents, they were on their way home and coming across New Mexico when their truck and the mobile home they were pulling got caught in a huge updraft and rolled them.

Both truck and trailer were totaled, and the contents of the trailer scattered over quarter of a mile of highway. It seemed as though everything was lost. But on taking a closer look at the side of the road nearest to where they were standing, they were amazed to see the box containing all their genealogy undamaged and intact!

It seemed like our ancestors were making sure those documents stayed with our family.

My maternal grandmother's name was Bradshaw. We had some information on the family, but nothing substantial.

About a year after my grandmother died, her brother Gene received a package labeled, "Gene Bradshaw." But when he opened the package, Gene realized nothing in it related to him, so he began searching for the rightful owner of the package, another Gene Bradshaw.

It turned out that this other man lived only twenty miles away in Beaverton, Oregon.

The two Genes got together and the package was delivered.

As the two men talked and compared family history, they eventually realized they *were* related. The second Gene Bradshaw is a Catholic whose Bradshaw research took him overseas to England.

Thanks to Gene and, I'm sure, to my grandmother's efforts on the other side, we were able to compile a book which included this missing part of our family history.

Dad Came to Us on My Mother's Birthday

Sarah Street Hinze, B.S., Author, Speaker, Educator, Therapist—
Arizona, USA

In October 1996, Mom asked me to visit her in Johnson City, Tennessee for her seventy-fifth birthday. She had the feeling this would be a very special day for her and wanted to share it with me. Dad passed away the previous year. Mom was doing okay, but she missed him so much. They had a great love affair for over fifty years.

I honored Mom's request and flew to Tennessee. I hadn't been home since Dad's funeral the previous November, and being in that house of memories where I grew up was harder than I expected. I was constantly aware of Dad's absence but determined to be cheerful for Mom's sake, so she could have a wonderful birthday.

It was also the weekend of General Conference. Saturday we celebrated Mom's birthday with friends and family. Sunday morning, I invited Mom to drive with me to the LDS Church and watch conference by satellite. She was not a member of the church and graciously declined my invitation.

I was happy that morning and excited to attend Conference. While driving my parent's old car to the chapel, I noticed a tape in the tape player. It was a Glenn Miller special—the only tape my dad ever purchased. As it began playing, I was suddenly immersed in one of Dad's favorites from the swinging big band sound of Glenn Miller.

It was like old times with Dad. Not surprisingly, I became emotional. Tears filled my eyes and waves of nostalgia rippled through me. I missed my father, but sensed something more. Then it hit me. With the spirit of discernment promised in my patriarchal blessing, I realized Dad was sitting next to me in the front seat of the car.

Feeling Dad's presence was a beautiful experience. Tears flowed—fast and full. It was difficult to see the road. I pulled two tissues from my purse to wipe my eyes. By the time I reached the chapel, the tissue was a wet ball in my hand.

I sat in the parking lot trying to understand. I'd learned through previous experience that when the spirit came, I needed to be quiet and meditate because a message was always delivered. I took out my journal, which I'd been impressed to bring for note taking during conference, then sat and waited.

I began to write as Dad spoke to my spirit:

"Sarah, I'm here with you. I want to attend conference with you. I've heard your prayers for me that I would be open to receive the missionaries. I've listened to the missionaries and am converted to the gospel. I want to be baptized into the gospel of Jesus Christ. I want Tadd (Dad's grandson) to do my work for me. I didn't understand the gospel when I lived on the earth. Those times you tried to teach me, I was afraid. I listened to the wrong people who steered me away. But now I know the truth and have a strong testimony. I want us to be an eternal family."

I was overwhelmed. That which I had ached for, prayed for, but hardly dared hope for, was happening on this special day.

Moist-eyed, I proceeded into the church and found a seat in the back of the chapel. I felt Dad still with me. Listening to the words of the Lord's anointed for the first time with my dad was a holy experience. Can you imagine my gratitude? And there was more. I continued to write impressions from him as I sat there.

There came a treasured love letter to me from Dad, followed by a final request:

"Sarah, go home and tell your mother what happened. I will be with you. I want you to go to your mother and *bear my testimony to her.*"

Again, I was overwhelmed. Dad wanted me to go home and tell these things to my mother? She would not understand. How could I do this? What would she think . . . that I had gone mad?

I cried all the way home. When I opened the front door, Mom was sitting in the living room waiting for me. I ran to her and said, "Mom, you won't believe what happened."

"Tell me!" she responded.

I told her everything. We cried. We hugged.

Finally, with tears in her eyes, she said, "I told you this would be a special birthday."

The next morning, I was preparing breakfast when Mom came out of her room. Her first words were, "What do I need to do to be baptized? If your dad's going to be a member of The Church of Jesus Christ of Latter-day Saints, then I want to be a member too."

More tears. More hugs.

We called the missionaries and they came to the house later that day. Mom took several missionary lessons before I left Tennessee. She arranged to visit our home in Arizona for her baptism. She also requested permission to receive her patriarchal blessing from our stake patriarch following the baptism.

A full year had passed since Dad's death by the time Mom arrived in Arizona. Our family went to the Mesa Arizona Temple and our son Tadd did the temple work for him. That evening, Mom was baptized by Rod, our eldest son. Afterwards, we joined in a family gathering at our home. What a celebration and special day for us all.

A few days later, Mom, my husband and I, and several of our children were sitting in the patriarch's front room, awaiting Mom's blessing. I offered a silent prayer. "Lord, I can feel my father here and I am grateful. But would you please bless a second witness to feel my father's presence too?"

The patriarch, Brother Davis, visited warmly for several minutes, then placed his hands on my mother's head and began the blessing. About halfway into it, he stopped. We all opened our eyes.

"Sister Street, something wonderful has happened that has never happened to me before in this capacity. Your husband is here and he is standing by my side. He has something to tell you. I will include it as part of your patriarchal blessing."

Words of love from my father to my mother began pouring through our Patriarch. I was startled as I heard these words. "Edna, I love you and our family very much. I want us to be an eternal family. I'm with our family here. Many of them have embraced the gospel. I have a strong testimony that it's true. When you pass over, we will teach more family members. But for now, enjoy your life and we will be together soon."

I was humbled. Some of the words and phrases that Brother Davis spoke for Dad were the same ones Dad spoke to me a short time before in Tennessee.

Then the patriarch reverted to his regular style and continued Mom's blessing.

Afterwards, Brother Davis told Mom, "That is the first time I've included a love letter from a spouse in a patriarchal blessing. Your husband loves you and your family so much."

Today, when asked about family history, my parent's conversion to the gospel, and my testimony of eternal families, I often respond, "Do you have a few minutes? Have a seat, and I'll tell you about a special gift to my mother on her seventy-fifth birthday."

An Old Brooklyn Newspaper

James Resseguie—New York, USA

Sometime around 1992 some friends and I attended a sports collectible show at the Nassau Coliseum on Long Island, where I was born and raised. I collect baseball cards and often attend such shows. We were at the show for about an hour, walking past hundreds of tables and booths, making a few small purchases here and there.

As my friends and I walked past one of these tables, I overheard two dealers talking. One said to the other that he recently purchased some 19th century newspapers from Brooklyn. I didn't know such papers still existed, never mind that they could be for sale at a baseball card show. I wanted to know what was in them. When I asked if I could see the papers, the dealer gladly obliged.

On impulse, I asked how much he wanted for them—twenty dollars for one. I couldn't decide which one to get, so he offered me both for thirty bucks, which I accepted.

When I first got the papers, I took them out occasionally to show friends, but then I pretty much forgot about them.

Some years later, I became interested in genealogy. It became a passion for me and still is today. While searching for my ancestors, I learned that for a time, my family lived in Brooklyn and owned an upholstery business there.

One night, I remembered those old newspapers and my family's connection to Brooklyn. I rummaged through my closet until I found the newspapers. After looking through the pages for twenty minutes, my eyes caught something familiar. There was an advertisement for Ressegiue's Patented Rollable Spring Mattresses.

I couldn't believe it! I had found an ad for my great-great-grandfather William F. Ressegiue's mattresses in 1852. Over the years, the spelling of *Resseguie* changed slightly, but it was the same family.

The ad was in only one of the two papers. If I hadn't bought both, I might not have picked the right one. If I had walked past that table at the card show twenty seconds earlier or later, I probably wouldn't have heard the dealer talking about them.

Years later, the *Brooklyn Daily Eagle* put their 19th Century archives on the Internet. It turns out the ad I saw appeared in a total of three issues. What were the odds I would find one of those three? Was it coincidence? Or did William F. Ressegiue have something to do with it?

Prompted to Miss Lunch and Search
Anne Hill—Utah, USA

Sarah Amelia Hey is my maternal grandmother and the daughter of James William and Lavinia Howarth Hey. My mother, Violetta Richards Schofield, believed her mother was an only child and knew nothing more about her parents than their names. For a long time, I searched fruitlessly for records on Ancestry.com to find more information. I was very discouraged.

Before giving up, I determined to visit the Family History Library of The Church of Jesus Christ of Latter-day Saints in Salt Lake City, Utah. As I walked through the doors, I prayed I'd be led to someone who could help me find my grandmother and her family.

When I entered the British research area, a gentleman jumped up from his chair to help—a missionary who appeared to be about seventy years old. The two of us searched in vain until it was time for him and his wife to take their lunch break. He promised me that *if* he had time between his afternoon assignments, he would help me further. I struggled on, finding no information at all in the 1881, 1891, and 1901 British censuses.

Ten minutes after he left for lunch, the gentleman missionary returned. He said, "I've been thinking about you and remembered looking through six hundred names on a British census before I finally found my own grandmother. I will do the same for your grandmother. I have decided to look through the six hundred names right now, before I go on to my other assignments." He immediately sat down at a computer and went to work.

About an hour later, he tapped me on the shoulder and whispered, "Come and see name number five hundred and sixty, which I've just read in the 1891 British Census." I felt a twinge of excitement.

The name on the screen was James William Hoy. I'd been told my great-grandfather's name was James William Hey. On the record, the wife was listed as Savinia Hoy. My great-grandmother's name was believed to be Lavinia. The couple had a one-year-old daughter, Sarah. My grandmother's name was Sarah Amelia Hey. The family was living where I expected to find them, and the date was compatible with my information.

In looking at the original census document on the screen, the O in *Hoy* could easily have been a mis-transcribed E—which would explain why I'd never found a family listed as *Hey*. Furthermore, the S in *Savinia* could easily have been an L, also mis-transcribed. Bingo!

The gentleman missionary and I searched further. We looked in the 1901 British Census in the same vicinity. He spotted a record for a William J. Hey who was living as a boarder with two little girls, Emma and Violet. William's age was appropriate for my great-grandfather, but there was no Lavinia and no Sarah Amelia listed with the family. I was speechless for a moment, and then tears filled my eyes. My missionary friend was surprised at my reaction, because the information did not look like anything we hoped to find. The reason for my tears was a highly significant name: Violet. It jumped right off the computer screen at me.

The missionary did not know that Sarah Amelia Hey had named her first daughter Violetta.

Violetta was also my mother's name, and I'd never heard of anyone else called Violetta. I'd wondered many times why Mother was named *Violetta* yet was always called *Violet* by her family. Now, I knew why.

I was sure we had found a record of her family. I was also sure my grandmother had two little sisters who needed finding.

I needed to know three things: Were Emma and Violet actually sisters of Sarah Amelia? Where was Lovinia, the mother of the little girls from 1901? And where was Sarah Amelia in 1901?

I sent for birth certificates for Sarah Amelia as well as Violet and Emma Hey. On each certificate, the parents were listed as James William Hey and Lovinia Hey, formerly Howarth. On her birth certificate, Violet's given name was listed as *Violetta*. I ordered a death certificate for Lovinia Howarth Hey, and I learned she died in a union workhouse in 1898, three years before the 1901 census was compiled.

As for Sarah Amelia: In the 1901 census, a Sarah M. Hey was listed as a *visitor* in the home of a Stephenson family, near the boarding house where James William lived with Emma and Violet.

An inspired and dedicated LDS missionary accomplished all this when he felt prompted to search through five hundred and sixty names instead of eating his lunch.

He Stayed with the Mail

Sherry Ann Miller, Author—Washington, USA

In 1985, my husband, Frank, and I visited Kalona, Iowa, where we ran into one of his cousins. She introduced us to another cousin, who took us to visit yet another cousin in a nursing home. At the home, they told us about a genealogical book *(Amish and Amish Mennonite Genealogies,* by Hugh Gingerich and Rachel Kreider) that had a massive collection of Frank's ancestors. Since Frank is of Mennonite and Amish descent, we were surprised to learn that these two religious groups are very diligent in recording their ancestral records. Naively, we once thought only Latter Day Saints were so involved in family-history gathering. Not so. We ended up buying the last copy of the book available at the time.

As we returned home, Frank and I discussed some of the names within the pages of the book, and I promised to help him gather his ancestors into a genealogical computer program and prepare them for temple submission. To my delight, I learned that I was one of the first persons to submit the names, so I made a goal to prepare one hundred per month. At that rate, I figured the project would take about twenty-five years, unless others started processing names as well. Most of the records came from city/county/state and census records and from over one hundred and thirty recorded family histories.

One day a month, I drove from my home in North Ogden, Utah, to the Family History Library in Salt Lake City. There, I searched the International Genealogical Index (IGI) for names entered that month to determine if any of my family names were previously submitted. For the first six or so years, I seemed to be the only person of Frank's many relations working on his line. After that, another Miller and a Yoder began submitting names, so the work progressed faster.

One night, while entering data on my computer, I had a spiritual vision of a great conduit open up outside my window, where thousands of people were waiting for their names to appear on my computer screen. As soon as I entered a name with its pertinent data and sources, that person would leave the line and another would slide into his or her position. As I viewed this vision, I could see the line of people stretching as far as the eye could see. I was impressed with the phrase, "Take a number. Stand in line," and realized for the first time how long many of these people had been waiting for someone to take their names to temples of the Lord.

It soon dawned on me that a hundred names a month was not going to be enough. That inspiration was given in a dramatic way. One month, I worked late into the night, trying to reach my one hundredth person. The hundredth name was a male ancestor, probably a distant cousin to my husband, who had lived in the late 1700s in Pennsylvania. I felt a keen urge to continue but was so tired that night I had to quit before I needed toothpicks to keep my eyelids open.

Retiring to bed, I kept thinking I should continue, but sleep soon overwhelmed the thought. However, around five in the morning, I awoke and felt strongly once again that I should finish the hundredth man's wife and children.

Obediently, I returned to my little den and looked up the last entry on my computer. He was the youngest son of a large family. I located his wives and children within the pages of the book. To my surprise, he had married thrice, his first and second wives having died at or shortly after childbirth. His children numbered seventeen between the three wives. As I entered the data into PAF, I felt the man's presence in my little den. Amazement filled me as I could spiritually see him in his Amish clothing, hat in hand, twisting it around anxiously as I worked. At one point I hit the wrong key, and heard him whisper, "Go back. There's a mistake."

He remained with those records as I searched the IGI and discovered that none of his family's names had yet been submitted. After I prepared them, I put them in an envelope and took it down the hill to the mailbox. I was not surprised to see him remain with the mailbox when I walked back to my home. Several times that same day I glanced out the window to see if the mail had gone, and each time, I sensed the man's presence. He was still on duty. When the postal driver picked up the envelope and took it away, the man went with it. I'm sure he remained with the packet until it arrived at the temple for processing.

This was a testimony to me of how diligently and carefully our ancestors watch over us as we prepare and process family names for temple submissions. It was also a teaching tool for me, and since that time, I learned not to limit myself, but to submit as many names as I could gather and verify.

Early in life, I assumed that most of my family's temple work was done. After all, Mama had come from a long line of stalwart Latter-day Saints. I was mistaken. The records that keep opening up year after year make me realize the work won't be finished in my lifetime. Nor my children's or grandchildren's. And there will always be family on the other side of the veil cheering us on. Always.

The Same Little Town

Alyson Bigelow Horrocks, Writer, Connecticut—USA

When we moved to Connecticut, I knew we had quite a bit of colonial New England history in my family. I excitedly began looking things up to see where in Connecticut and Massachusetts my ancestors had lived. I found it fascinating that I could actually go to places where my family lived three hundred years ago.

A year after moving, we searched for a town to buy a house, as we were in a rental. Russ and I both fell in love with Simsbury—such a quaint, small town, surrounded by forested hills and lush vegetation. The town does a fantastic job of keeping its historical character, which really appealed to me.

From the moment we found our house in Simsbury, we felt like we were home, and that we'd been drawn to this place.

Earlier, I asked my father-in-law if they had any family history in New England. He told me no, but I didn't believe him. Not that I thought he was lying, just that he didn't know. He'd traced only the Horrocks line, and they came to America in the 1900s. He didn't know anything else about the other lines, and we all descend from hundreds of lines.

Shortly after settling into our home in Simsbury, I was tracing a particular line on my father's side and, to my surprise, I found family in the 1600s living in Simbury. Abigail Phelps was born here, and Phelps is a big name in this town, even to this day. I was thrilled.

A few days later, I was looking into my husband's lines. Turns out that he does, in fact, have many ancestors from New England. He is even descended from William Bradford of the Mayflower, governor of Plymouth Colony.

I kept tracing my husband's lines and suddenly found one of his ancestors named Mary Phelps, born in Simsbury, Connecticut. *How strange*, I thought. I then compared our lines—Abigail and Mary Phelps were sisters!

Not only did I discover that my husband and I were related, descended from the same line, but the place where our lines met was Simbury, our new hometown. It gave me chills because we both truly felt drawn here. What were the odds we would end up in this town on the east coast, when my husband is from Utah, and I'm from California?

We always joke that Abigail and Mary were behind all this, but I really do feel they had something to do with it.

A Civil War Dream

James W. Petty, AG, CG, B.A., B.S., Professional Genealogist—Utah, USA

I used to work for a man named Derek Shadel who wanted to identify his ancestors and provide temple ordinances for them. I am what I call a lucid dreamer; meaning I am aware of my dreams and can often remember them when I awake. I even catalog my dreams and can chose a particular theme to dwell on when I close my eyes. I can also interact in my dreams, making choices of my role in the dream.

On one particular night, however, I began dreaming randomly and became aware that I was standing on a bluff overlooking a Civil War battlefield. As I watched, I saw men yelling, guns firing, and cannons booming out their destruction. In the midst of this scene, Two soldiers climbed the hill where I stood. They approached me, and one of them introduced himself, saying, "We are Derek's Grandfathers." Nothing else was said, but I had the overwhelming feeling they wanted their temple ordinances done.

I woke up and made a note. It was about 3:00 AM. The next morning, I called Derek Shadel and related the experience to him, asking him how many of his grandfathers served in the Civil War. He called me back to say all eight of his 2nd great-grandfathers had served. Together, we searched LDS temple records and discovered that of those eight men, two did not have their temple work done.

Needless to say, the two men became the focus of our research efforts, and within a few months, the ordinance work for those men and their wives and children was complete.

The Fabulous Shutts
Elizabeth Aiton—Canada

When I was a child, a framed drawing leaned against a wall in the attic. The drawing was created in 1899 from a photograph taken of my great-grandmother Martha Shutt about 1850. This drawing always fascinated me, because I resembled Martha.

Martha Shutt

Later, I left England to live in Canada, and asked my father if I could take the drawing of Martha and a matching one of her husband with me, as no one else in the family was interested in them. He agreed, and they hung in my dining room for years.

I constantly wondered about Martha.

Despite my fascination with her, I never researched the Shutt line.

One day, I had the strong feeling I should telephone the assistant registrar at my old hometown in County Durham, northeast England. She had been extremely helpful on previous occasions, and although the rules were that one should not telephone the office and speak with employees regarding family-history research unless it was to order a certificate, I felt I really needed to talk to this lady.

During the course of our conversation about other things, I happened to mention my paternal great-grandmother's surname, Shutt.

I was shocked to hear the assistant registrar say, "Oh, the Shutts! The fabulous Shutts."

It turned out that when she was in training, she had to select an unusual name and research it as far back as she could go. She chose Shutt.

This lady was able to send me information going back to my great-grandmother's great-grandparents, including their children and spouses. She also passed on information given to her by other genealogists with whom she had shared this research regarding children, grandchildren, and their spouses.

Following the inspiration to make the telephone call brought Martha and her family a step closer in my life.

She Did Belong!

Victoria Heighton Firth, Librarian—Utah, USA

Several years ago, I searched to prove that one of my husband's ancestors (Melvina Ellis, born 1827, Westfield, Richmond, New York) really was part of her family. Nothing showed her as a member of the family, and she didn't appear in census or church records. However, I had a strong feeling Melvina belonged to the Ellis family.

One day, determined to find the proof I needed, I prayed on my knees in the morning before going to the Family History Library in Salt Lake City, Utah. I prayed in my heart the whole way there and then while there.

I did some research and then felt prompted to look at the will for the man I believed was Melvina's father. I got the microfilm, put it on the reader, and started going through Garrett Ellis's will. And there it was: Melvina's name, as one of his daughters.

I started crying and wanted to jump up and down doing the happy dance. I felt comforting arms around me and realized Melvina was with me. It was so wonderful to know she wanted this work done as much as I did, and a very humbling feeling to know she had guided me.

Tears still come to my eyes as I relive this experience. Afterwards, I was able to find increasing amounts of information for this family. It was amazing.

A Google Miracle

Tamera Westhoff—Kansas, USA

A branch in my family history completely stopped because a girl named Mary Tamar Lowe married her first cousin, Daniel Fielder Lowe, in North Carolina in 1784, and we had no idea who her parents were.

While researching my family in the Family History Library, I spent most of the time every month looking for this girl's parents. Her middle name was almost the same as my first name, so I felt a kinship with her.

After years of research, I had notes full of information, but nothing on Mary Tamar Lowe.

I married and had children, and for many years there was no time for family-history research.

Then one day, my mom asked if I ever found Mary Tamar Lowe's parents. I replied that I hadn't. I went straight to the computer and Googled *Mary Tamar Lowe*. Up popped a link to the Rootsweb site, naming Thomas Lowe as Mary's father. It felt like a miracle.

Random Question
Shirley Rothas—Florida, USA

My maternal grandfather had an older brother named Ambrose Herbert Chappell (born November 1877, Chowan County, North Carolina) whom I knew was married to a woman named Carrie.

I found a website containing information on many members of my family. Some of it was incomplete, so I wrote to the owner of the site and shared what I knew. He immediately wrote back and asked if I knew anything about James Davis, listed on the 1930 census as Ambrose's brother-in-law.

I wrote that James Davis must be Carrie's brother-in-law, but as I went to click SEND, someone clearly told me, "No, he's not. You need to look."

"Look where?" I asked, but the only thought that came was, *Look harder.*

So I did, and found that Uncle Ambrose was married twice before he married Carrie. He married Anne E. Reath (born April 1882, Pennsylvania) in Wilmington, Delaware, in 1903. Witnesses for the wedding were Anne's sister and brother-in-law, Mary and James Davis. Anne died, and Ambrose married Mae A. Campbell (born 1883, Pennsylvania) in 1914 in Wilmington. Mae died in 1919 and Ambrose married Carrie B. McComsey (born 1892, Pennsylvania) in 1922.

I thought it was interesting that both James and Ambrose were widowed and remarried, but they remained close and even lived together in 1930.

Why would someone who isn't closely related to my family ask about a vague person on a census, when there were so many other questions he could have asked me? No one in my family ever mentioned Uncle Ambrose marrying three times. My mother probably didn't even know, as he married Carrie before Mom was born. I never would have thought to look for other wives.

I haven't asked the owner of the site why he asked the question, but I believe he was inspired to do so because I needed to find these aunts and complete their work in the temple.

A Father's Heart Turns

Diane Evans, M.S. ASQ, Certified Software Quality Engineer—
Washington, USA

My paternal grandfather died tragically in 1917 when my father was three months old. His mother could never bring herself to talk about her late husband. When my father was twenty, she, too, passed away. Knowing nothing about his father—having never even seen a picture of him—left a large hole in his heart.

In the early 1970s, I received enough information from my mother's family to complete the maternal side of my four-generation pedigree chart.

My father's side, however, was a big blank. I dropped to my knees and prayed, "Thou gave this commandment to complete a four-generation sheet. I know the Lord gives no commandments unto the children of men that cannot be accomplished. Please help me find the information I need."

Years passed. When I found my grandmother's obituary in the early 1990s, I discovered she had a half-brother named Paul whom my dad had forgotten about. Paul was orphaned at a young age, so I went to the archives in Tacoma, Washington, to see if I could glean any information from the probate records.

All the county records were recorded on microfilm. I found it, got the information I was looking for, and went back to the desk. As the clerk reached for the microfilm, I suddenly drew it back and said, "I'm not done with this yet."

I put it back on the reader and found my grandparents' marriage record. There, in black and white, were the names of my great-grandparents: Richard Otte and Helena Smits.

I still didn't have any other information, although I knew my grandfather was born in New Jersey. I struggled again to find more about them. Miracles came in bits and pieces. I found a city directory with a Dirk Otte listed. Since my uncle Dick's real name was Richard, it seemed likely the same thing might apply to a great-grandfather.

I had a powerful witness that this was indeed my great-grandfather, a feeling that turned out to be correct. My great-grandfather's name was Dirk when he came to America. He Americanized *Dirk* to *Dick*, but other people always assumed, in error, that *Dick* was short for *Richard*. Even my grandparents' marriage certificate listed *Richard* Otte instead of *Dirk* Otte as Leonard's father.

However, the burial record does have the correct name, Dirk Otte. In 2000, I finally discovered why I was unable to find the family in the 1880 census—the last name had been misspelled. Someone recorded it as *Oode* instead of *Otte*.

My father passed about in May 2001, still wondering about his father. About nine months after his death, I got an email from a man saying, "I think we are related." It turned out that his great-grandfather was my grandfather's brother. I told him about the misspelling of the last name, and he gave me information I didn't have.

We soon traced the family to the late 1500s in Holland.

I wanted so badly to tell my father about this miracle of family history so he could finally find out about his father's line. Then I realized that my father already knew; the first thing he must have done when he got to heaven was track down his father then find a way to get the information to me.

A Root Trip

Heather Wilkinson Rojo—New Hampshire, USA

When my daughter was little, she loved to help me search for tombstones in graveyards all over New England.

It is always good to have a second pair of eyes when the burial ground is big, especially when you have no idea where someone's stone is located. My daughter also had a mysterious connection with my Munroe ancestors—an uncanny knack of finding them. This never happened in any other graveyards, or with any other ancestors.

Once, when my daughter was very small, we drove all the way from home in New Hampshire to Peabody, Massachusetts. Typical of a young child, as soon as we found the graveyard she announced she had to "tinkle." I told her to run behind some trees while we looked for a certain grave.

When she returned, she asked me who we were looking for, and I showed her the name spelled out on a card. She started to giggle, and we immediately knew where she had tinkled.

A few years later, we attended the re-enactment of the Battle of Lexington, Massachusetts. We walked over to the nearby burial ground to photograph some other gravestones. We were looking for several surnames, but I really wanted to find the gravestone of George Munroe, our immigrant ancestor from Scotland.

We photographed many stones then called to our daughter to return to the car. She ran to join us, tripped over a root, and when she looked up—guess what name was right in front of her. We joked that perhaps it wasn't a root, but that maybe Great-Grandpa Munroe was reaching out to her.

Don't Stop Now

Linda Weaver Clarke, Author
with Alan Kelly Weaver (siblings)—USA

My mother was doing some genealogy and came to a stop. She didn't know where to go next. That night, she began to doze off, when she felt the presence of people in the room. On opening her eyes, she saw the room filled with her ancestors, and she sensed they were pleading with her to keep searching. My mother understood this was a message given to her for a purpose and knew her ancestors would help her.

The following morning, Mother took my brother, Alan, recently returned from a mission, to the genealogy center and began working. She handed him a book and asked him to search for Dorothea Gotherson from Salem, New Jersey, who married John Davis. Mother knew Dorothea died on 28 September 1709, in Salem, New Jersey, and that she was from England, born 13 July 1661, but that was it.

Alan took the book and began searching. Before long, he found Dorothea's name, with all her information, including her parents. Dorothea was born in Godmershem, Kent, England. Now my mother knew exactly where to begin. Dorothea's parents' names were Daniel Gotherson and Dorothea Scott, from St. Alphage, Kent, England.

With this information, my mother grabbed another book, began searching, and was then able to connect to other ancestors. Before she realized what was happening, a bunch of names seemed to leap off the page—she had discovered generations and generations of names connected to the Scotts.

What a magnificent find. Mother was grateful for that prompting to keep searching.

Saved from the Mice

CathyAitken Summersell—Yorkshire, England

How I got started on family history amazes me. My father was a great genealogist who loved it very much. He tried sharing it with me, but I wasn't interested. Not that I didn't want to do it; family history just puzzled and confused me, and I didn't know how anyone found the time.

In 1997, I traveled to my friend's wedding in my hometown, where my father still lived. His bishop came up and mentioned he was concerned about Dad's health. He suggested I visit Dad before returning home.

During that visit, Dad and I chatted for a couple of hours. He shared with me his testimony of the Gospel and gave me a large brown envelope containing the family history he'd done on both his and my mum's side. He especially asked me to continue this great work and hoped it would bring me pleasure.

Sadly, three weeks later, Dad passed away. I knew I should continue the work he'd started, but family, home, and work got in the way, and time went by. The envelope ended up in the attic without even one attempt at further research.

Then one day, I heard scurrying and scratching in the attic. I opened the attic trap door to find mouse droppings everywhere I looked. I began clearing the attic and was horrified to find that everything made from paper had been shredded and used by the mice to make nests—everything except for one last item, which I brought downstairs: the brown envelope containing all my father's genealogy remained untouched.

That blessing should have been another signal for me to carry on Dad's great work. But no. Eight more years passed, and all I did was think about it.

Then my sister, passed away in October 2008 at the age of forty-eight. That was the day I finally took note of what was happening.

My older brother and I were the only active family members in the LDS Church, so we put together a funeral service that would bring the family together and help us keep in touch.

Since then, genealogy has been an important part of my life. A dear friend had the patience to help me begin, and I haven't stopped since.

I've felt the presence of my parents while doing the work. There have also been times when I've woken up in the early hours and been given guidance to find names of new families belonging to my tree.

What a blessing it is to be part of this great work here on the earth today.

The Right Time
Alie Vermeer—Netherlands

One day while in The Hague National Archive, I decided to search for more information about my great-great-grandmother, Pietertje Pons.

It was a terrible day. Everything went wrong. The film I needed was missing and books that could help were not available. I decided to look for information on another branch of my family tree instead and come back for Pietertje some other time.

A couple of weeks later, I went back to the same archive and started searching again for Pietertje Pons. This time, the film and books were available—but not readable.

I went for a third time, and yet again, I couldn't find Pietertje.

I became frustrated and went to a quiet place in the Archive and offered a silent prayer. I asked that if Pietertje didn't want her temple work done, to let me know one way or the other.

It was made clear to me she didn't want to be found yet, as she needed more time. So I kept her in my thoughts.

A few years later, I was in the Archive searching for another family.

While walking toward one of the bookcases, I suddenly felt myself being gently guided in the opposite direction, toward a bookcase on the other side, and I forgot which book I was looking for.

This happened three times, and I eventually thought, "Okay, if this is it, then so be it." I looked up, picked a book at random, and let it fall open.

There was Pietertje Pons with three generations of her ancestors. Then I started crying.

I did Pietertje's temple work as soon as possible. I felt her presence while doing the ordinances on her behalf, and grew close to her in the process.

Pietertje Pons made *genealogy* turn into *family history* for me.

A Familiar Voice

Tom Baker—Washington State, USA

I was working in my home office when I heard a familiar voice calling, "Tom!" It seemed to be coming from down the hall, in the living room.

Immediately, I answered "Yes?" and stood up. Looking out the window to my left, I saw my wife, Kathy, who had just arrived and was standing a few feet from the school bus she drives. I wondered how I could hear her voice in the living room when she was standing in the front yard.

Who else could be calling me? I felt as though I knew the voice well. Then I realized it was my mother. How could this be? She'd passed away thirty-five years ago.

When Kathy walked in and said, "Hi," I knew for sure it hadn't been her voice that I heard.

Even so, later that evening while lying in bed, I had to ask, "Did you call me this afternoon when you were standing by the bus?"

Laura Mecham Baker

She said she did not. I knew then I really *had* heard my mother's voice. The reason was for me to discover.

Kathy and I had talked earlier in the week about going to the temple, as I knew I had work to turn in and complete. Little did I know how important it was that we followed through with this commitment.

The next day, I was working at my computer, when something prompted me to open the temple work briefcase Dad left for me. As I opened it, a warm feeling came over me. I reached in the back pocket and pulled out a blue floppy disc labeled "Tom Baker Family Backup." I looked in the front compartment and pulled out my great-great-grandma's family information.

Seattle Washington Temple

In the same pocket I found another copy of the "Tom Baker Family Backup." This one had the name crossed out, and "Temple Ready" written over it.

On Friday, Kathy and I took the disc to the Seattle Temple and handed it to the sister at the family names desk. When

she printed the information, only one name appeared. Sarah Taylor, my great-great-grandmother, needed to be sealed to her parents. The rest of the family work had already been done.

As we did the work for Sarah, tears filled my eyes, and I could see in my mind her picture on the living room wall—the room from where I heard Mom call out my name earlier in the week.

Sarah Taylor

I understood how important Sarah Taylor's sealing was to her parents for time and all eternity.

We're Related

Betty Butler—USA

My husband and I were team teachers of genealogy as well as ward record examiners. I worked a short time on our stake pilot project of extracting names from Spain. This was back in the dark ages of the 70s and 80s before computers and the Internet.

In one class, we taught a new family who had just moved in. They brought the wife's Book of Remembrance to class. As I walked past the table, I glanced at several tintypes, an old photography method from the 1800s with the image displayed on small pieces of glass and encased in a hard folder with a fold over lip.

I stopped, stunned at the images. "I have those same pictures. Who are they?" She flipped previous page over for me to see her family group sheet.

"Those are my grandmother's grandparents," I said.

It turned out we were cousins three times removed, and we could help each other with research. She had records of an uncle of my grandmother's, someone I had only sketchy information on. He was the man who held the pay for the Mormon Battalion as they came thru New Mexico. He took the money the soldiers earned back to their families in Nauvoo or elsewhere. I later found this man, his wife, and sister on the records of the Nauvoo 3rd Ward, and his wife on the original Nauvoo Relief Society rolls.

When my cousin went home to tell her children what happened, her little daughter exclaimed, "That's why their kids were so nice to me in Primary when no one else would help me find my class. We're related."

A Great Trip

Leeann Boone—Wisconsin, USA

I'd pretty much given up finding anything on my great-grandmother's stepmother, Emma Ross and her family. All I knew was that Emma's mother was Lois Babcock, and her grandmother was Miranda Babcock. Beyond that was a dead end.

One day, I was visiting Prairie Home Cemetery in Waukesha, Wisconsin with my dad, as we have several family members buried there. We made the rounds, and when my dad returned to the car, I ventured off to visit a few more graves.

On my way back to the car, something amazing happened. That particular area of the cemetery is uneven, and I was used to watching where I step so I don't fall over any broken stones. This time, I wasn't careful enough, and I tripped right next to a weathered gravestone.

I stopped myself from falling to the ground then ended up gazing in disbelief at the words on the gravestone.

The name engraved was Munson E. Babcock, born 1894. Perhaps this was a relation to Miranda Babcock, Emma's grandmother. After staring for a few moments, absorbing this information, I ran back to the car and we drove home.

I immediately researched Munson Babcock and discovered that he and Emma were first cousins.

After finding this grave, I was able to get a lot of information on Emma's Babcock line.

Hundreds of Family Bibles

Tracy St. Claire—Illinois, USA

At first glance, it seemed my interest in genealogical research happened by accident, but now I think the odds of that are impossible. I was meant to find my family Bible.

I stumbled on the Bible while looking for something else on eBay, but somehow a particular listing came up despite what I was searching for. I remember looking at the title of the item and recognizing *Wolverton* as one of my major family lines. So I clicked on the link, and as I read, I slowly understood that these were *my* Wolvertons, containing ancestor connections I did not know about.

The seller described its origin, "I rescued this Bible from a barn in Central Pennsylvania, on the edge of Dutch Country. The Bible had apparently been in that barn for scores of years, in a trunk which had not been opened, judging from the dust on the Bible. It was published in 1838 by R.P. Desilver of Philadelphia. The barn was owned by a couple of Dutch bachelor brothers who had accumulated an amazing collection of family heirlooms and antiques of every description in their small home. In fact, I'm told the last of the brothers slept on the floor, because the bed and everything else in the house was covered in antiques."

I bought the Bible for $183, but frankly, I would have drained my checking account and credit card to get that Bible. It had belonged to my great-great-great-grandparents.

Finding the Bible wasn't particularly unusual, and wouldn't be now, when you can configure eBay to e-mail you whenever "Wolverton Bible," or any word or phrase is on a current auction. What was unusual was what happened afterwards. Since I hit the genealogy jackpot, my outlook on the odds related to this find were greatly skewed. I was convinced I could easily find more of my family's Bibles if I looked.

I started accumulating Bibles, usually with my family surname (but in later years not), looking for direct or collateral relatives. One thousand two hundred Bibles later, I did not find another hit. I posted the contents of over half of these books at my site (www.biblerecords.com) but still retain an enormous library of other people's ancestors.

No. Finding the Bible was not an accident. I feel certain of that.

From Jew to Christian

Rochelle Rose Blakeslee Beach, Professional Crafter—Idaho, USA

My Jewish grandmother Gussie Schnieder (née Tiechler) and I were very close when I was a little girl. Gussie was born in Manhattan, USA, and her husband, Benjamin was from Austria.

Gussie died at age fifty-four when I was eleven. One evening many years later, after retiring to bed for the night and drifting off to sleep, I was awakened by a disturbing dream.

Grandmother Gussie came to me, pleading with such sadness—why didn't I get her family-history work done for her? Not having it done obviously caused her pain, because her face looked distorted. It was a startling dream. I could not bear to think I caused my grandmother any pain at all.

As soon as possible, I completed her work[1]. This brought me peace, and I have the strongest feeling my wonderful, loving and beautiful Jewish grandmother accepted the Gospel of Jesus Christ.

[1] Family members of Jews can do temple work for their Jewish relatives.

A Danish Miracle

Patti Miner, Singer Songwriter—Utah, USA

When one of my grandmothers died, she left my Uncle Darel some Danish records in the family Bible. Uncle Darel was more of a father than an uncle to me. He raised me and was the only member of the LDS church in his family of Lutherans. He was also one of the most perfect men I have ever known. I loved his family. They were kind, soft-spoken peacemakers, and God-fearing people.

Because Uncle/Dad Darel was eighty-nine, he was unable to do family history work, so he gave the records to me. But they were written in Danish. I called around to find someone who could translate it for me, but could not find anyone.

So I took my GED-COM files to the local family history center and began chatting with the women who worked there. The worker normally came on a different day but was filling in for someone else. She overheard our conversation about my Danish records and said she spoke the language and would love to translate them for me. It turned out she was the mother of one of my best friends. What a blessing.

I ran home and got the records. Within two days, this lady and her husband had them translated, typed up, and delivered. It was all family history with family lines, names, dates, and places. What a gold mine!

Most of the family was from Kegnaes, Denmark, so we ordered the Kegnaes Parish microfilm from the Salt Lake City library. The record arrived a week later, just as I finished entering all the information from the translated records into my home computer.

When my friend put the microfilm on the machine, she was disappointed because it was written in Old Danish, which she didn't understand.

We sat there, dejected, for a few minutes. Then another worker came in from the next room and asked what was wrong. We explained the problem, and she remembered a lady who recently died had donated quite a few books to the library. One pamphlet was entitled, *How to Read Old Danish Parish Records*. Wow! Who knew such a thing existed?

Within a few minutes, my friend began translating, and I recorded the words as she spoke. We couldn't believe all the information—two-page obituaries with names of parents, spouse and parents and children. The pastor had written some wonderful things about family individuals. It was amazing. We could feel what a great and goodly people these were.

Later, when my friend told another genealogist about our find, he said we were lucky to have death records from that date and location as they weren't always available.

While doing the work in that large, empty room, we both had the overpowering feeling that there were many more people present.

Once, as we went through records, we both spoke aloud in unison, "I know, I know, we'll go back," as if answering a woman we'd skipped one page earlier and she was bugging us about it.

We both smiled and looked at each other and said, "Who were *you* talking to?"

Over the next three weeks, we recorded nearly three hundred names connected to the early 1600s.

One amazing discovery while doing this work was realizing that my great-grandmother, Cathinka, had died three days before I was born. When I was very small, I named all my dolls Cathinka, and my parents couldn't understand how I came up with such an unusual name out of the blue.

I think I must have promised Cathinka, during those three days in heaven, that I would one day complete her family history work for her on earth.

It took several years of submitting the family names to the temple, printing cards, and asking friends and family to complete the work. When I gave the completed book with all the family lines and completed temple dates to Uncle/Dad Darel, he cried with such tender joy.

He died two months later. I know he went back a hero to his family.

Information in a Mess

Julie Cloward—Maryland, USA

When I lived in Utah some years ago, a teacher in church enthusiastically encouraged me to get involved in my family-history research. I was Primary president at the time, and life was busy. Besides which, I thought my grandmother had done it all.

However, this teacher didn't give up. She kept calling and inviting me to visit the family-history library to at least check the system and see how everything worked.

Finally, I agreed to go. As I looked up my father's side of the family— the Petersens—it seemed the research was done, the work complete.

I then searched for my mother's ancestors and soon discovered the information to be a mess. Many names were misspelled, and my grandfather Yearsley was not listed as married to my grandmother. I was shocked and left the library, heading for my car, determined to ask my mother about these mistakes.

As I sat behind the steering wheel, pondering the situation, I suddenly felt the presence of my grandfather right beside me in the car. The thought came clearly, "You need to sort this out for me. I love your grandmother and want to be with her for eternity."

When I told my mother what happened, I was even more surprised when she asked me to leave things the way they were.

After considering it further, Mother hired a genealogist to sort out her side of the family, and eventually their temple work was done. I felt her parents' joy when that happened. They had waited a long time.

Fruitful Connection

Stephanie Huss Rask with Sher Huss (siblings)—Utah, USA

My sister Sher and I went to the Bountiful Cemetery to take photos of headstones that belonged to our Mom's family. When we entered the cemetery office, Sher told the woman who worked there our family name—Marshall—and asked for help locating headstones.

The woman, Annette, became excited and astounded us by saying, "That is the family line I am working on this week."

When Sher asked Annette if she was working on any particular name in the Robert Elijah Marshall family, she said, "Ann Sinclair," because she was convinced there were two of them but didn't know for sure.

My sister told her there *were* two Ann Sinclairs—a mother and a daughter. The mother was Ann Campbell Sinclair. The daughter was Ann Sinclair Scott Marshall. Sher then shared the story of how Robert Marshall and the two Ann Sinclair's met.

My sister happened to bring a pedigree chart with her that day, and when Annette looked it over, she pointed to Edwin C. Pace's mother—Edwin was our great-great-grandfather—and immediately said, "This is my great-great-great-grandmother!"

Annette then gave us a story about Edwin C. Pace that was written at his death. And she gave us a copy of our grandfather's death certificate, which solved a mystery as to what caused his death.

It was amazing to Sher and me that all three of us descendants of the Marshall family were at this cemetery at the same time and on the same day. This was a fruitful connection for each of us.

Dreams and Voices

Sally Mace—Utah, USA

My father had just passed away. As I walked into his office after the funeral, I noticed his scriptures were open on his desk. I wondered what he had been reading. Then an overwhelming feeling came over me, and I felt the spirit of Elijah fill my soul. I knew dad wanted me to work on his genealogy.

I searched out one of our family genealogist on Dad's side and began working with her. A month later, I had a dream in which my father came to me. I told him I was surprised to see him, and he told me if I would continue doing my genealogy, he would be with me.

For the next two years, I was able to do the work and feel my father by my side. Even in my dreams, I would see him standing there smiling at me. The love I felt from him was amazing.

My family then moved to a small town, and I was unable to continue the work for several years. I haven't seen my father in my dreams since the move.

However, I'm sure Dad knew when my research continued and rejoiced with other ancestors, because one day, while in the Salt Lake City Family History building, while searching through the film drawers for family names, I felt impressed to pull out a drawer for which I didn't have a number. I put the film on the reel and searched through it.

I was amazed to see family names toward the end.

It was then I heard a male voice say, "She has found us!" The voice was full of emotion. I could feel the presence of several people and a witnessed a feeling of great joy and happiness. I looked around—there was no one else in my aisle. I was alone. I got goose bumps all over me and was very excited.

Later, I asked my brother to take the names of the males to the temple. While he was doing the baptism for one of them, he asked for the proceedings to stop because something was wrong.

The gentleman who was saying the names said, "Yes, I feel the same thing."

My brother then said, "He wants his name pronounced this way." With that correction, they were then able to continue.

After all the baptisms were done, my brother was getting ready to go home, when he heard a voice say, "Please finish my work now." My brother recognized the person who wanted his name pronounced correctly, and with feelings of great joy obtained permission to complete the work.

Not Given to Flights of Imagination

Randy Lindsay, Security Specialist—Arizona, USA

In the early part of 2008, I finally decided to begin working on my family history. My family converted to the LDS Church when I was young, but had not done much research.

I happened to visit my father around that time and mentioned that I was working on our family tree. He immediately told me he'd recently been seeing images of people when he went to bed at night. These were men and women of all shapes, sizes, and description. They wore what my father described as "old time" clothing. Although none of them spoke to him, a large number paraded past his vision.

My father said that he didn't know any of these people, but thought the visions must be a silent appeal to have their genealogy done. The visions were persistent, and he encouraged me to be diligent in my research.

Frankly, I was surprised to hear this from my father. He's a very grounded individual and not given to flights of imagination. If he claimed to have seen faces of the departed, then I had to believe that it was happening.

Over the next several months, I made great strides in my research. I tracked the majority of my father's side of the family back to about 1850 and never expected the work could be as exciting and rewarding as it was.

Next time I met with my father, I rattled off my discoveries about our family. Then I asked him if he still saw those faces. He said they stopped a little while after our last talk together and never returned.

We are both convinced the visits were from our ancestors who hoped our generation would search for them and complete their temple work.

I look forward to the time when I can meet the people I've come to know through my efforts in researching family history.

About the Author

 Although born in Wales, Anne Bradshaw grew up in England and now lives in the USA. When not glued to the chair typing, she is reading, working on family history, walking, or enjoying photography. Anne and her husband Bob are parents to four children, and grandparents to fourteen.

True Miracles with Genealogy is Anne's sixth published book. It will soon be available as an eBook for all electronic readers.

Visit the website for *True Miracles with Genealogy* at **www.truemiracleswithgenealogy.com**, where all are welcome to submit inspiring stories about miraculous events relating to their research. If your story fits, Anne will edit it and post it to the site for public reading.

Anne's Blog—annebradshaw.blogspot.com
Anne's website—www.annebradshaw.com
Facebook—www.facebook.com/anne.bradshaw
Twitter— twitter.com/AnneBradshaw